Stories from My Mother

A Cookbook of Memories

Madelyn Craig & Jeanette Mills

Rosewood Publishing

ISBN: 978-1-7355711-4-0 (Hardcover)

ASIN: B0CFSTV638 (Ebook)

Rosewood Publishing

www.madelynrosecraig.com

Table of Contents

Breads, Biscuits, and Baked Goods **173**

Introduction

Hello, friends. Let me tell you a story.

My mom loves to cook. Now, you might have heard, "My mom likes to bake stuff on occasion for friends and family." But that is not what I said. I said my mom loves to cook. And bake. And create. She is truly an artist in the kitchen. Unfortunately, she takes Picasso's view a little too seriously and breaks all the rules. In fact, it can be a bit difficult to find an actual recipe for something she has made. Or rather, it was. But after much lamenting and pestering from her friends and me, here we are.

My mom likes the phrase "cooking by the seat of my pants." She does most things this way, for better or worse. She likes to create, experiment, taste, and share with others. She loves putting on a full spread, another phrase I have heard many times. But most of all, I think she simply likes to make stuff, especially for people. She inherited this love from my grandfather. He loved to cook. My grandmother did not cook… or should not have. My mom would often tell me stories of her and her siblings smelling spaghetti cooking on the stove when they came home. They loved spaghetti because that meant spaghetti and eggs the next day. But before they got too excited, they checked the top of the sauce. They could tell instantly who had made the dish before them and whether or not it would be enjoyable (or edible). Thus, it was my grandfather who taught my mother to cook. Although, she picked up a few things herself along the way. I suppose my mom and I are the same in this way.

My mother was also a cake decorator. I do not mean she made pretty cakes for the kids, family, and friends. I mean she was a professional, an artist. And in many cases, she made EXACTLY what the client wanted (for better or worse). I will never forget the teal sponged cake with white and yellow flowers, the candy cake with the most unique toppers, or the art deco cake that was very...art deco. Hey, the customer is always right, right? But my mom was a master in the kitchen and the bakery.

She was so good that she and my dad opened a sweet shop called Sweet Expressions in Wyandotte, MI. Even after they closed, my mom kept on creating. Unfortunately, that love did not pass on to me. Well, not at first. Until I was married, I did not like to cook OR bake. I would not even touch raw meat with my bare hands. There are many reasons for that dislike, but over the years, I have come to enjoy cooking and baking for my family. And like my mom, I love to create. I paint, I write, I sculpt, and now I bake and cook. But cooking is not like the other arts. Cooking is the art of creating something that will not last because it nourishes others. Baking is the art of creating something unique and delightful that brings joy and comfort. Both involve a basic knowledge of rules and a hint of experimentation. Many of those experiments led to this book.

My mother is the main artist here, but I wanted a little something of her art and mine to last longer than our memories. There is a lot about our past that we do not know or remember. But a little something that has spanned at least four generations is cooking, and that is something I want to pass on to you and my children. I have mixed emotions when it comes to cooking, but in the end, I have come to love it. Most of all, it is a way I connect to my mom and her life. And so, I give you this book to use, to read, and to enjoy for years to come.

There is a little bit of me and my mom between these pages. So, take our recipes and our stories and enjoy them as you make some of your own. Bake with your family; share a dish with a friend! Make memories together.

These are stories from my mother, a cookbook of memories.

~Madelyn Rose Craig

Before You Begin

Before you get out your ingredients, I want to offer a couple of tips and share a bit about this book. First, get out all of your ingredients before you begin! This will hopefully save you from finding yourself halfway through a recipe only to discover that you do not have vanilla or parmesan cheese (I would not know anyone this has happened to, but I have heard of such things). Second, you will notice that I do not always give servings. This is because I have found most serving suggestions incredibly subjective. I can turn two chicken breasts into eight to ten meals. For someone else, that might be four or two. Third, I have included cook times within the recipes as estimates for how long the actual cooking or baking times should be, barring whether you have a cool oven or like to fire-brew everything. But prep will take as long as it takes you. For example, it should only take me a half hour to make chocolate chip cookies, but if I am making them with my children, it will take me at least an hour. Perhaps you have a small kitchen or a large one. Perhaps you have a finicky stove, or three small, ravenous beings that demand your every moment, thus dividing your time between answering their questions on when they will have sustenance and making said food properly. So, take those estimates as just that. Finally, begin with the end in mind. Clean as you go. Consider when a meal needs to be done, how long it takes to cook or bake, and how quickly you can gather ingredients. I find this helps reduce meal preparation time immensely. With that said, get cooking and enjoy!

Breakfast

Morning Traditions

Between the moments of sleep and wakefulness, as the sun crept through the space of the window and curtains, while half of the world was already meeting the day's tasks and the other wouldn't meet them for an hour or two more, the scent of buttered eggs, warmed tomato sauce, and toasted bread met a waking face. It is morning, and it is time for breakfast. But not just any breakfast: spaghetti and eggs.

There was a moment's pause as the child sifted through thoughts and dreams and scents, deciphering between the real and the hope. She sniffed again. Yes, this was real. She listened and leapt from the bed. The sound of scraping pans and a ticking toaster greeted her ears. Her dad was home, it was morning, and breakfast was nearly done.

Racing past the bathroom that waited with her combs for the mop atop her head, she arrived at the doorway of the kitchen. A tall, stooped back greeted her, the arms mixing and stirring and doing what they loved best: making food. Well, perhaps that was a second love. Their first love was planting, but not this morning. This morning was for breakfast, and she was here for it.

Perched atop a stool opposite the counter, Joey watched her dad finish the eggs and warm the leftover spaghetti. It was not the meal for everyone. Most people were fine with hot sauce, or some other tomato-based condiment, but not spaghetti. Noodles with eggs? Why? Because that is how her dad made it, and you know what, it was good. Steam rose from every surface, filling the room with warmth and welcome. Her dad looked over his shoulder, shrugged, and gave a hint of a smile before returning to his work. Nothing was said overtop the bubbling of the butter and sauce on the stove, but this was comfort. No words were needed.

In a moment, a plate of spaghetti and eggs sat before her and another before him. Quietly, they ate their breakfast together at the counter. The sun was continuing its circuit, but neither her brother nor mother had woken up. And it was unlikely they would anytime soon. That was how the mornings went, and that was ok. The morning would soon be over, and with it would come the weekend. Then the weekend would end, and Monday would come again when she went to school and her dad to work, when tiredness would creep through his legs to his back and his head would sink lower until it found something to numb the days.

But not today. Today was for little traditions with her dad. Today was spaghetti and eggs and toast, which had finally made it to her plate to clean up the remaining sauce. Today was for quiet moments, moments with Dad.

Apple Cinnamon Oatmeal

Cook Time: 10 min.

Ingredients:

- 2 ¼ cups water
- 1 large apple, peeled and diced
- 2 cups rolled oats
- ½ tsp salt
- 2 tsp ground cinnamon
- ⅓ cup raisins
- ⅓ cup walnuts, chopped
- milk
- brown sugar or honey

Instructions:

1. Bring water to a boil in a medium saucepan and add apples.
2. Boil for 3 minutes.
3. Reduce heat to medium-low and add oats. Cook for another 4 minutes, or until oats have absorbed all the water, stirring continuously.
4. Turn off the stove and add salt, cinnamon, raisins, and walnuts.
5. Portion out into bowls and add milk and sweetener.

Baked Oatmeal

Temp: 350°F   **Cook Time:** 30 min.

Ingredients:

- 3 cups rolled oats
- 1 tsp baking soda
- ½ cup brown sugar
- 2 tsp ground cinnamon
- 2 eggs, beaten
- ¼ cup butter, melted
- ¾ cup milk
- ½ cup water
- 2 cups fruit
- honey or syrup

Instructions:

1. Grease a deep 9x13" baking dish.
2. Preheat oven to 350°F.
3. In a large bowl, mix oats, baking soda, brown sugar, and cinnamon.
4. In a separate bowl, combine eggs, butter, milk, and water.
5. Pour the wet mixture into the dry mixture and stir.
6. Mix in fruit.
7. Pour the mixture into the baking dish and distribute evenly.
8. Bake for 30 minutes or until the center is firm.
9. Remove from oven and serve with honey or syrup.

Bread Pudding

Temp: 350°F

Cook Time: 45 min.

Ingredients:

- ½ loaf thick bread or rolls, stale
- 1 tsp ground cinnamon
- ⅓ cup raisins
- 3 tbls butter, melted
- 1 ¼ cups milk
- ½ cup heavy cream
- ½ cup sugar
- 3 eggs, beaten
- ½ tsp vanilla extract

Vanilla Sauce

- 6 tbls butter, melted
- 2 tbls brown sugar
- 2 tsp vanilla extract

Custard Sauce

- ½ cup heavy cream
- ½ tsp cornstarch
- 1 egg yolk
- 2 tbls sugar

Instructions:

1. Preheat oven to 350°F.
2. Dice bread or rolls into large chunks and place them in a greased 9x9" baking dish. Dust with cinnamon and raisins.
3. Melt butter in a medium mixing bowl and whisk in milk, cream, and sugar. Mix in eggs and vanilla.
4. Pour the milk mixture over bread and bake for 45 minutes.
5. You can make either the vanilla sauce or the custard sauce.
   a. For the vanilla sauce, whisk together melted butter with brown sugar and vanilla.
   b. For the custard sauce, whisk together cream and cornstarch in a small saucepan. Add in egg yolk and sugar and bring to a simmer and whisk for 3 minutes. Remove from heat and let cool.
6. Remove pudding from oven, top with sauce, and serve.

Breakfast Sausage

Cook Time: 15 min.

Ingredients:

- 2 lbs. ground pork
- 2 tsp salt
- 1 ½ tsp pepper
- 2 tsp dried sage
- 1 tsp dried thyme
- ½ tsp dried rosemary
- ½ tsp marjoram
- 1 tbl brown sugar
- ½ tsp paprika
- ½ tsp red pepper flakes
- ¼ tsp ground nutmeg

Instructions:

1. In a small bowl, whisk all the spices.
2. Place the ground pork in a large bowl and add all the spices.
3. Using your hands or a fork, work all the spices into the pork.
4. Once well combined, refrigerate for at least 30 minutes to allow the flavors to meld.
5. Form meat into twelve 2" patties or crumble into a large fry pan.
6. Cook at a medium heat for about 15 minutes or until browned.
7. Drain on paper towel and serve or freeze.

Buttermilk Biscuits

Temp: 450°F   **Cook Time:** 12-15 min.

Ingredients:

- 3 cups flour
- 4 tsp baking powder
- ½ tsp baking soda
- 1 ½ tbls sugar
- 1 ½ tsp salt
- 12 tbls butter, cold
- 1 ¼ cups buttermilk, cold
- 2 tbls honey
- 1 tbl butter, melted

Instructions:

1. Preheat oven to 450°F and line two baking sheets with parchment paper.
2. Whisk together all dry ingredients in a large, wide bowl.
3. Using either a pastry cutter or a food processor, cut cold butter into the flour mixture. The butter should be grain sized.
4. Mix milk into the flour mixture to form a sticky dough.
5. Roll out dough on a floured surface to about 1" thick.
6. Using a biscuit cutter, cut out 16 biscuits (lift, do not twist cutter) and set 2" apart on parchment-covered baking sheets.
7. For long-term storage or if your butter has gotten soft, set them in the freezer until the biscuits are firm. Then either place them in zip lock bags or onto the counter.
8. Mix honey and butter and brush biscuits.
9. Bake in oven for 12-15 minutes, or until golden.
10. Remove and serve with butter or jam.

Corned Beef Hash

Cook Time: 40 min.

Ingredients:

- 3 tbls olive oil
- 3 tbls butter
- 6 cups potatoes, sliced
- 12 oz. canned corned beef

Instructions:

1. Warm butter and oil to a medium-high heat in a large fry pan.
2. Peel and slice potatoes. Add to fry pan.
3. Once the potatoes are just starting to brown, add corned beef in small chunks and mix it into the potatoes.
4. Continue frying until potatoes and meat are crispy. Be careful not to overcook and burn them.
5. Flip regularly.
6. Once the hash has finished cooking, scoop a 1 ½ cups of hash onto a plate and serve with scrambled or over-medium eggs.

Eggs a la Eddie

Cook Time: 30 min.

Ingredients:

- 4 medium potatoes, diced
- 4 tbls butter
- ½ small yellow onion
- ½ lb. diced ham or cooked breakfast sausage (p. 12)
- 10 eggs
- 1 cup milk
- 1 cup cheddar cheese, shredded

Instructions:

1. Peel and dice potatoes.
2. Add potatoes to a large fry pan with the butter.
3. Once potatoes are golden brown, dice and add onion and meat to the pan and cook for a few more minutes.
4. While the potatoes, onions, and meat finish cooking, mix eggs and milk in a separate bowl.
5. Once the potatoes are ready, add the egg mixture and stir.
6. Once the eggs have finished cooking, top with shredded cheese and serve.

Egg and Sausage Strata

Temp: 350°F   **Cook Time:** 1 hr.

Ingredients:

- ½ red pepper, chopped
- ½ cup yellow onions, chopped
- 2 tbls butter
- 1 lb. breakfast or mild Italian sausage
- 4-6 slices bread
- 2 cups cheddar cheese, shredded
- ¼ tsp salt
- ¼ tsp pepper
- 8 eggs
- ¾ cup milk

Instructions:

1. Cook and break up sausage in a fry pan. Drain, and set aside.
2. Sauté peppers and onions in butter. Add to the sausage.
3. Cube bread slices and layer in a greased 10" square baking dish.
4. Layer sausage mixture over bread.
5. Sprinkle with cheese.
6. Whisk together milk and eggs and pour over bread, sausage, and cheese.
7. Let the dish sit for 20 minutes before baking. Alternatively, cover and refrigerate overnight.
8. Preheat oven to 350°F.
9. Bake for 35-40 minutes until the center is firm and serve.

Buscia's Farmhouse Quiche

Temp: 375°F **Cook Time:** 1 hr.

Ingredients:

- ½ lb. bacon
- 1 small yellow onion, diced
- 10 oz. spinach, chopped
- 1 cup sour cream
- 1 cup parmesan cheese, shredded
- 2 cups ham, diced
- 2 cups cheddar cheese, shredded
- 1 cup Monterey Jack cheese, shredded
- 10 eggs
- 1 ¼ cups half and half
- ¼ tsp salt
- ¼ tsp pepper
- 2 unbaked pie crusts (optional)

Instructions:

1. Cook bacon in a medium fry pan until crispy. Remove bacon and set aside.
2. Preheat oven to 375°F.
3. Sauté onion in bacon grease until onions are translucent.
4. Add in thawed, drained spinach and cook for 3 minutes.
5. Transfer to a medium bowl and stir in sour cream and parmesan cheese. Divide and spread spinach mixture in the bottom of two pie crusts or pie pans.
6. Layer each quiche with ham, bacon, and cheese.
7. Beat eggs with half and half, salt, and pepper. Pour the egg mixture over the meat and cheese mixture.
8. Bake for 45 minutes and serve.

Quiche Muffins

Temp: 350°F   **Cook Time:** 35 min.

Ingredients:

- 2 tbls butter
- ½ cup potatoes, diced
- ½ cup broccoli, diced
- ¾ cup ham, diced
- ¾ cup cheddar cheese, shredded
- 10 eggs
- ¼ tsp salt

Instructions:

1. Preheat oven to 350°F.
2. Fry potatoes in butter until soft in a small fry pan.
3. Steam broccoli for 2 minutes in the microwave until al dente.
4. Grease a 12-cup muffin pan lined with muffin papers.
5. Layer potatoes, broccoli, ham, and cheese in each of the muffin cups.
6. Whisk eggs and salt in a large bowl and ladle into the muffin cups.
7. Cook in the oven for 20 minutes.
8. Serve immediately or cool, freeze for about an hour on a parchment-lined baking sheet, and freeze in gallon freezer bags.
9. Thaw one in the refrigerator overnight and reheat for 1-2 minutes in the microwave.

French Toast

Cook Time: 30 min.

Ingredients:

- 1 loaf Amish white bread (p. 175)
- 6 eggs
- 1 cup half and half or heavy cream
- 1 tsp vanilla extract
- 1 tbl ground cinnamon
- butter
- maple syrup or honey

Instructions:

1. Whisk together eggs, half and half, vanilla, and cinnamon in a wide and shallow bowl.
2. Heat a skillet or fry pan to a medium heat and grease with butter.
3. Dip slices of bread into the egg mixture and lay in greased skillet or pan.
4. Fry each side until golden, about 4 minutes total.
5. Remove from pan and top with butter and honey or syrup.

Oatmeal Bran Muffin Tops

Temp: 350°F   **Cook Time:** 20 min.

Ingredients:

- 1 cup butter, softened
- 1 cup brown sugar
- 3 eggs, beaten
- 1 cup flour
- 2 cups rolled oats
- 1 ½ cups bran
- 1 cup walnuts, chopped
- 1 ½ cups apples, chopped
- ½ tsp salt
- 1 tbl baking powder
- ½ tsp ground cinnamon

Instructions:

1. Preheat oven to 350°F.
2. Mix wet ingredients in one large bowl. Mix dry ingredients in a separate bowl.
3. Combine the dry mixture into the wet mixture.
4. Divide dough evenly into 16 portions and roll into balls.
5. Stagger 8 balls on each baking sheet, spacing them about 2" apart, and gently press each ball down to about 1" thick.
6. Bake two sheets at the same time for 12 minutes. Rotate the cookie sheets top to bottom and front to back and bake for another 8 minutes.
7. Remove from oven and set onto the stove.
8. Let cookies set for a few minutes on the baking sheets before serving.

Pancakes

Cook Time: 15 min.

Ingredients:

- 2 cups flour
- 4 tbls sugar
- 3 tsp baking powder
- ½ tsp salt
- ½ tsp ground cinnamon (optional)
- 1 ¾ cups buttermilk
- ½ tsp vanilla extract
- ¼ cup butter, melted
- 2 eggs
- 1 ½ cups berries or chopped fruit (optional)

Instructions:

1. Whisk together dry ingredients.
2. Add in milk, vanilla, and butter. Mix until just combined.
3. In a medium bowl, separate egg whites. Put yolks in mixture.
4. Beat egg whites into firm peaks either with a whisk or hand mixer. This should take about 2-3 minutes. Set egg whites in the refrigerator and let the batter sit for 10 minutes. This step can be skipped, but the pancakes will be less fluffy.
5. After 10 minutes, fold in egg whites.
6. If desired, add fruit.
7. Pour batter onto a greased, medium hot skillet.
8. When bubbles rise and pop on the surface, flip over.
9. Cook the second side until golden.
10. Serve with fruit topping, syrup, or honey.

Almost a Recipe, But Not Quite

Two heapers, an egg, and enough milk to thin it up.

That's it.

That was the recipe for what we call Polish Pancakes. It's not much, is it? And yet, that is the recipe we lived by for decades in our family. So, what is a heaper? Basically, you take a soup spoon and scoop a "heaping" mound of flour. Then, you add an egg. And how much milk? Well, make it like a thin pancake batter. It will not get puffy like a pancake. Instead, it should be thin and smooth enough to flow over a greased pan. Like a crepe.

As a kid, I honestly thought my grandpa made this recipe up. We called them Polish pancakes because that is what my mom said her dad called them and he was Polish. We had all assumed he had come up with the recipe, or maybe, maybe, his mom made it up. But we called them *Polish* pancakes nevertheless because, well, what else could we call them?

But one fall, as I was looking up various Polish foods for my upcoming "Polish" Thanksgiving (I was craving some pierogi and gołąbki), I stumbled across something called naleśniki. I had not seen this word before, so I looked into it. I was not sure I could trust the pictures, so I looked at the recipes. Sure enough, they were quite similar to what my grandfather had taught my mother (but with the typical measurements you'd use for cooking!). I could hardly believe it. Polish pancakes had a real name! They really were *Polish* pancakes! Though suffering from a game of telephone (and loss of the Polish language in our family), this little dish actually connected us to our roots in Poland. I was so excited, I told my whole family. Sadly, they did not find my revelation quite as amazing.

While I still use the original instructions when I make my Polish pancakes (because who *really* measures when making treats?), I decided we needed a more formal recipe of my grandpa's making. So that is what you have here. No heapers, a more accurate measurement of "enough milk to thin it up," and an egg. You have naleśniki, a thin pancake that made its way across Europe and the Atlantic with a little Polish family who made it to America. These pancakes may have lost their original name along the way, but the memories and delight they bring have stayed.

Naleśniki (Polish Pancakes)

Cook Time: 15 min.

Ingredients:

- ¼ cup flour
- 1 egg
- ¼ cup milk
- butter
- jam (optional)
- bacon, chopped (optional)

Instructions:

1. This recipe is best doubled or tripled if made for more than one person.
2. Whisk together ingredients into a thin, smooth batter.
3. Melt butter in a fry pan at a medium-low heat.
   a. Alternatively, place pieces of bacon in the pan.
4. Pour batter into the pan until you have about a 6"-8" disk, depending on the size of the pan.
5. Quickly rotate the pan to spread the batter around to form a very thin pancake.
6. Fry until the pancake is golden on the bottom and flip.
7. Fry for a couple of minutes on the other side. Both sides should be a golden color.
8. Remove from heat.
9. Place a dollop of jam in the center of the pancake.
10. Roll the pancake and enjoy.

Sausage Gravy

Cook Time: 20 min.

Ingredients:

- 1 lb. breakfast sausage (p. 12)
- 2 tbls butter
- ¼ cup flour
- 2 cups milk
- ½ tsp pepper

Instructions:

1. In a medium fry pan, cook and crumble breakfast sausage over a medium heat. Drain fat into a safe container.
2. Add butter and sprinkle flour over the sausage, stirring with a wooden spoon.
3. Slowly add milk, one cup at a time. Stir continuously while cooking over a medium heat until all milk has been added.
4. Continue to simmer for about 5 minutes or until gravy is at the desired thickness.
5. Serve over biscuits.

Stuffed French Toast

Temp: 350°F   **Cook Time:** 1 hr.

Ingredients:

- 1 loaf bread (10 cups cubed)
- 2 cups blueberries
- 2 tsp ground cinnamon
- 8 oz. cream cheese
- ⅓ cup sugar
- 1 tsp vanilla extract
- 10 eggs
- 1 ½ cups milk
- ¾ cup maple syrup or honey
- 6 tbls butter, melted

Instructions:

1. Grease a 9x13" baking dish.
2. Cube bread and put ¾ into the baking dish.
3. Evenly distribute blueberries over bread.
4. Sprinkle cinnamon over bread and blueberries.
5. Melt and combine cream cheese, sugar, and vanilla.
6. Drizzle cream cheese mixture over the bread.
6. Cover with remaining bread cubes.
7. Mix the remaining ingredients and pour over the bread.
8. Cover and set in the refrigerator overnight.
9. Preheat oven to 350°F.
10. Bake uncovered for 1 hour.
11. When the center is fully cooked, remove from the oven and serve.

Waffles

Cook Time: 20 min.

Ingredients:

- 3 cups flour
- 4 tsp baking powder
- 1 tsp salt
- 1 ½ cups buttermilk
- ½ cup water
- ¼ cup butter, melted
- 1 tsp vanilla extract
- 4 eggs
- ½ cup sugar

Instructions:

1. Mix flour, baking powder, and salt in a medium bowl.
2. Add in buttermilk, water, butter, and vanilla.
3. For the eggs and sugar:
    a. Separate yolks from whites. Add egg yolks to the batter. Beat egg whites in a separate bowl to stiff peaks. Fold egg whites into the rest of the batter with sugar.
    b. Or, beat eggs and sugar in a separate bowl with a hand mixer for 1 minute. Then fold into the rest of the batter.
4. Heat up a waffle maker, grease both grids, and pour enough batter to cover one of the grids.
5. Cook until waffles are golden and remove from the waffle maker.
6. Serve with fruit topping, syrup, or honey.

"Stuff" and Surprises

I like to make surprises for people. Not just surprise them, not just make them something, but to make surprises. There is a joy in the creation and the opportunity to see the person receive their surprise, and the best is always food. One night, I was making a surprise for the morning, a breakfast surprise. It was going to be such a coup. The only problem was that the person whom the surprise was for, my mother, was sitting in the adjoining room. And I was MAD at her. Looking back, I cannot even remember why. I cannot remember a single word that was spoken, or what the argument was about. Regardless, I did not want to see her, let alone make something for her. But tomorrow was Mother's Day, so there I was, quietly and furiously searching for and mixing ingredients.

My family is not one for gifts, or surprises really. Gifts are found last minute, cards are absent, and there is nearly never a surprise for what a gift will be. I sometimes think this is because my mom hates buying "stuff," and this because my grandmother loved it. Her house was filled with "stuff." Not many objects with memories, nor special, precious things (save the few I deemed special enough to keep), but there was "stuff." Boxes, shelves, and mounds of "stuff." Sometimes, that "stuff" ended up with us.

When I was about eight years old, I remember one such bag of "surprise stuff" arriving at our house. It was summertime, and the day was bright and warm, though my brother and I had yet to venture outside. We heard a loud blare of a horn and ran to the front window. A Grand Marquis was parked in the driveway, and my grandma's disheveled head poked out the window. Thinking back, I can see her smile. I cannot remember if she actually smiled that day — I doubt it — but that is how I usually remember her. This is not to say she was always happy, but around us, she usually smiled. The blare of her car horn sounded again, just before my mother was able to open the door and see what she wanted.

"Hey, mom. What's up?"

"I got some stuff in the trunk for the kids." My grandma was always to the point when she wanted to be.

As my mom went to the back of the car, my grandma unlocked the door so she could open the trunk. Out popped two giant black garbage bags, large enough to belong to Santa but cheap enough to be from Walmart. My mom lugged them towards the house and then went back to her mom.

"Do you want to come inside and see how the kids liked what you got them?"

"No. I gotta get home to your father."

Then as though the house might be on fire, she backed out of the driveway and sped home. I mean that. You will never see another person maneuver a car so quickly or so recklessly (I hope not, at least). We would watch her speed away and then go to see what goodies she had brought for us, or what my mom permitted us to have at that moment. My mom does not like "stuff," remember, let alone "surprise stuff" that she had to sift through. But she does like food and making it for people. It is how she often shows her love.

So, on that Mother's Day Eve, I was making her food and hating it all the way. I'd tried waiting her out, hoping she'd go to bed before I started so it could be a surprise, but I needed to sleep. Whatever. Breakfast is breakfast, so who cares? I angrily sliced the bread and layered it in the pan. I pointedly sprinkled cinnamon and mixed milk and eggs. I huffily searched for vanilla, fuming for a moment, realizing I would soon need to ask for my mom's help. I had been noticeably quiet this whole time, trying to make sure she did NOT know I was making HER anything. But I could not find this crucial ingredient. I searched through a couple more cupboards (why was nothing where it should be?). Nothing. I had to ask her.

"Hey, where is the vanilla?"

"It's in the cupboard on the left. Why?"

Why, indeed, do mothers always know where things are? I found the vanilla. "I'm making something."

"What are you making?"

"…...Something for breakfast."

"Why?"

I knew the game was up. I had to tell her.

"For Mother's Day."

She asked no more questions after that, so I was able to continue taking out my anger on the sugar, cream cheese, and vanilla. But at this point, it was an act, and I knew it. You see, when you take the time to make something for someone, surprise or not, it is really hard to be angry at them. For there is love in making things, the best things, anyway. Your time and energy go into them as your hands move and mix and create. How can you hate someone while making them stuff?

I knew the surprise had been ruined, my quiet irritation to no avail. But my gift would be good, the "stuff" appreciated, and in the new day, I would get to do what my grandma never did with "surprise stuff:" spend time with her and see how she enjoyed it.

Main Course

Chicken Bake

Temp: 350°F   **Cook Time:** 45 min.

Ingredients:

- 2 lbs. chicken breasts
- 1 lb. broccoli, chopped
- 10.5 oz. cream of chicken soup (p. 329)
- ¼ cup water
- 1 tbl garlic, minced
- 1 ½ cups cheddar cheese, shredded
- ½ cup breadcrumbs

Instructions:

1. Preheat oven to 350°F.
2. Cut chicken breasts into 8-10 pieces or strips.
3. Lay in a 9x13" baking dish.
4. Spread frozen broccoli over chicken.
5. In a small bowl, mix soup, water, and garlic.
6. Pour over broccoli and chicken.
7. Top with shredded cheese and breadcrumbs.
8. Bake for 45 minutes.
9. Remove from oven and serve.

Baked Chicken Enchiladas

Temp: 350°F   **Cook Time:** 20 min.

Ingredients:

- 21 oz. cream of chicken soup (p. 329)
- 8 oz. green chilies, chopped
- 1 cup sour cream
- 1 ½ lbs. (4 cups) cooked shredded chicken or ground meat
- 12 small soft tortillas
- 3 cups Mexican cheese, shredded

Instructions:

1. Mix soup and chilies in a medium saucepan over low heat, stirring frequently.
2. Mix sour cream into the soup mixture and remove from heat.
3. Spread ½ cup of the soup mixture in the bottom of a 9x13" baking dish.
4. Set ½ cup of the soup mixture aside.
5. Add cooked and shredded meat to the remaining soup mixture.
6. Preheat oven to 350°F.
7. Divide chicken and soup evenly among the tortillas and roll with 2 tbls cheese. Place in the 9x13" pan on top of the soup.
8. When all the tortillas have been rolled, cover them with the rest of the soup mixture and the remaining cheese.
9. Bake for 20 minutes until the cheese is hot and bubbly.
10. Remove from oven and serve.

Cheesy Rice Casserole

Temperature: 375°F   **Cook Time:** 20 min.

Ingredients:

- 3 cups broth
- 1 ½ cups basmati rice
- olive oil
- 2 chicken breasts
- 2 tbls garlic, minced
- 3 tbls butter
- 3 oz. cream cheese

- ½ cup sour cream
- ½ tsp dried basil
- 1 tsp salt
- 4 cups (1 lb.) broccoli, chopped
- 1 ½ cups cheddar cheese, shredded

Instructions:

1. Boil rice in the broth until broth is completely absorbed.
2. Preheat oven to 375°F.
3. Add enough olive oil to coat the bottom of a medium fry pan and add the chicken breasts. Cover and cook until the internal temperature reaches 165°F.
4. In a large frypan, heat and combine garlic, butter, cream cheese, and seasonings to form a creamy mixture.
5. Add rice and broccoli to the mixture.
6. Chop chicken and add to the mixture along with 1 cup of cheese.
7. Place in a 9x13" casserole dish and top with remaining cheese.
8. Bake for 20 minutes.
9. Remove and serve.

Chicken Fettuccine Alfredo

Cook Time: 30 min.

Ingredients:

Alfredo Sauce
- ½ cup butter
- 5 oz. cream cheese
- 2 cups milk
- 2 tsp cornstarch
- 1 ¼ cups parmesan cheese, grated
- 1 egg, beaten
- 1 tbl garlic, minced

- 1 tsp salt
- 1 tsp dried basil

Breaded Chicken
- 2 chicken breasts
- ½ cup panko crumbs
- ½ cup parmesan cheese, grated

- 16 oz. fettuccine

Instructions:

1. Melt butter and cream cheese in a medium saucepan.
2. Mix cornstarch into milk and pour into the saucepan.
3. Once the milk is hot, whisk in parmesan cheese.
4. Once the cheese is mixed in, whisk in the beaten egg.
5. Add garlic, salt, and basil.
6. Simmer and stir for 5 minutes until the sauce begins to rise in the pan. Then immediately remove from heat.
7. Cover and set aside until ready to serve.
8. Slice chicken into ½"x2" pieces and coat in panko and parmesan mixture.
9. Fry in olive oil at a medium heat in a large fry pan for 5 minutes on each side, or until golden and the juices run clear.
10. Drain on paper towel and set it in a warm place.
11. Boil noodles in salted water until they are al dente.
12. Portion out noodles, sauce, and chicken and serve.

Chicken Marsala

Cook Time: 40 min.

Ingredients:

- 1 ½ lbs. chicken breasts
- ¼ cup flour
- ½ tsp salt
- ½ tsp pepper
- 3 tbls olive oil
- 2 tbls butter
- 8 oz. mushrooms, sliced
- ¼ cup onions, minced
- 2 cloves garlic, minced
- ⅔ cup chicken broth
- ½ cup Marsala wine
- ⅔ cup heavy cream
- 2 tsp thyme, chopped
- 2 tbls Italian parsley

Instructions:

1. Slice chicken breasts in half and flatten to ¼" thickness.
2. Add flour, salt, and pepper to a large zip-top bag.
3. Add chicken and cover with the flour mixture. Set aside.
4. Heat oil in a large fry pan to medium-high.
5. Shake excess flour off chicken and place in pan, cooking until each side is golden, about 5 minutes. Set aside on a plate.
6. Add butter and mushrooms to the pan. Cook until mushrooms are brown, about 4 minutes.
7. Add onions and garlic and cook for 2 minutes.
8. Add broth, marsala wine, heavy cream, and thyme to the pan, scraping the pan and incorporating all ingredients.
9. Bring to a quick boil then lower to a simmer and reduce the sauce by half. It should thicken and darken in about 10-15 minutes.
10. Add chicken and lower the temperature.
11. Cook for another 3 minutes, sprinkle with parsley, and serve.

Chicken Nuggets

Temp: 350°F   **Cook Time:** 30 min.

Ingredients:

- 2 lbs. chicken thighs or breasts
- ½ tsp garlic powder
- ½ tsp onion powder
- 1 ¼ tsp salt
- ¼ cup flour
- 3 eggs, beaten
- 1 cup cornstarch or flour
- 3 cups crushed cornflakes or panko crumbs
- olive or canola oil

Instructions:

1. Cut off fat and dice chicken.
2. If desired, brine or marinate in milk or pickle juice for 1 hour.
3. Place chicken pieces in a food processor and puree.
4. In a large bowl, mix the chicken puree with spices and flour.
5. Heat 2" of oil to 350°F in a large saucepan.
6. Scoop out 1 tbl of the meat mixture, roll into a ball, and flatten into a small patty about a ½" thick.
7. In a small shallow dish, beat the eggs. In two separate shallow bowls, set aside the cornstarch and breading.
8. Take the chicken patties and dip them first in the cornstarch, then in the eggs, then in breading.
9. Fry in oil for about 5 minutes until golden and internal temperature reaches 170°F.
10. Drain on paper towel, cool, and either serve or freeze.

Chicken Penne

Cook Time: 3-6 ½ hrs.

Ingredients:

- 1 cup chicken broth
- 21 oz. cream of chicken soup (p. 329)
- 1 tsp dried basil
- ½ tsp salt
- 3 tbls garlic, minced
- 1 ½ –2 lbs. chicken breasts

- ½ cup sour cream
- 2 cups cheddar cheese, shredded
- ½ cup parmesan cheese, grated
- 1 lb. penne pasta

Instructions:

1. Add broth, cream of chicken soup, basil, salt, and garlic to a large crockpot and stir together.
2. Add chicken breasts.
3. Cook on LOW for 6 hours or HIGH for 3 hours.
4. Bring a large pot of water to a boil.
5. Once the chicken is fully cooked, start boiling the pasta al dente. Do not overcook.
6. While the pasta cooks, shred the chicken in the crockpot.
7. Add in drained pasta, sour cream, and cheese.
8. Combine thoroughly and cook for another 15-20 minutes.
9. Turn off the crock pot and serve.

Pizza Chicken

Temp: 350°F   **Cook Time:** 30 min.

Ingredients:

- ½ cup panko crumbs
- ⅓ cup parmesan cheese, grated
- ½ tbl dried basil
- 1 tsp salt
- olive oil
- 4 large chicken breasts
- 1 cup pizza or pasta sauce
- 1 ½ cups mozzarella cheese, shredded

Instructions:

1. Preheat oven to 350°F.
2. Mix panko crumbs, parmesan, basil, and salt in a flat, wide dish.
3. Warm oil to a medium heat in a large, oven-safe frypan.
4. Slice chicken breasts in half.
5. Cover chicken in breading.
6. Fry the breaded chicken until the breading is golden brown and the juices within run clear, about 10 minutes total. Do not overcook.
7. Spoon two tbls of sauce onto each breast and then spread across the top of the chicken. Sprinkle with shredded mozzarella.
8. Set pan in the oven for 20 minutes or until cheese is golden and chicken has an internal temperature of 170°F.
9. Remove from oven and serve.

Chicken Salad

Ingredients:

- 2 boneless chicken breasts
- 1 stalk celery, diced
- 1 medium gala apple, diced
- ½ small red onion, diced
- 2 tbls lemon juice
- ½ cup dried cherries
- 10-15 seedless grapes, halved
- ½ cup walnuts, chopped
- ⅓ cup plain yogurt
- ⅔ cup mayonnaise
- ½ tsp salt
- ¼ tsp pepper

Instructions:

1. Place chicken breasts in an oiled fry pan and, at a medium heat, cook until they reach an internal temperature of 170°F. Alternatively, use the breasts from a cooked rotisserie chicken.
2. Remove from heat and cube chicken breasts.
3. Place in a large bowl in the refrigerator to cool.
4. Once the chicken has cooled, toss with celery, apple, onion, and lemon juice.
5. Combine thoroughly with cherries, grapes, walnuts, yogurt, mayonnaise, and spices and serve.

Chicken Tenders

Temp: 350°F   **Cook Time:** 30 min.

Ingredients:

- 4 chicken breasts
- ½ cup flour or cornstarch
- 3 eggs, beaten
- ½ cup parmesan cheese, grated
- ¾ cup panko crumbs or breadcrumbs
- ½ tsp salt
- 1 tbl garlic powder
- olive or canola oil

Instructions:

1. Slice chicken breasts in half and then into ½" thick strips.
2. Set flour or cornstarch in a wide shallow bowl. Beat eggs in another bowl. In a third bowl, whisk parmesan, breadcrumbs, salt, and garlic powder.
3. Fill a medium pot with 1-2" of oil and heat to 350°F.
4. Coat chicken strips in flour, then eggs, then in breading mixture.
5. Fry a few pieces of chicken in oil for about 5 minutes until juices run clear. The internal temperature should be at 170°F.
6. Set on paper towel to drain and serve.

Geode Surprise

Temp: 350°F   **Cook Time:** 30 min.

Ingredients:

- 8 chicken breasts
- 16 slices cheese
- 16 slices (½ lb.) ham
- 1 cup flour
- 1 tsp salt
- 2 tsp garlic powder
- 1 tsp dried basil
- 3 eggs, beaten
- 2 cups panko crumbs

Sauce:
- 2 tbls butter
- ½ tbl garlic, minced
- 2 tbls flour
- 1 cup milk
- 2 tbls Dijon mustard
- ½ cup parmesan cheese, grated
- ½ tsp salt

Instructions:

1. Cut chicken breasts in half horizontally. Pat dry, cover with plastic wrap, and flatten to ¼" with a mallet or rolling pin.
2. Layer with cheese and ham, roll, and close with a toothpick.
3. Heat a deep pot with 3" of oil to 350°F.
4. Stir flour and spices in a shallow bowl. Whisk eggs in another shallow bowl. Add panko crumbs to a third shallow bowl.
5. Dredge chicken rolls in the flour, then eggs, then panko crumbs.
6. Fry in oil for 5 minutes per side until the breading is golden and the chicken (not the filling) reaches 165°F.
7. Meanwhile, melt butter in a small saucepan at a medium heat. Add garlic and flour and whisk for 1 minute. Add milk and whisk to a smooth texture while bringing to a simmer.
8. When the mixture is thick, add mustard, parmesan, and salt.
9. Remove the chicken from oven, drizzle with sauce, and serve.

Oven Roasted Chicken

Temp: 350°F

Cook Time: 20 min/lb.

Ingredients:

- whole chicken
- olive oil
- 1 tbl salt
- 1 tbl garlic powder
- 1 tbl dried basil
- ½ tsp pepper

- (2) 12 oz. beer or ginger ale cans

Brine

- ¾ cup salt
- 1 gallon water

Instructions:

1. Remove any giblets and the neck from the chicken and brine the chicken for 4-12 hours in the refrigerator.
2. Preheat oven to 350°F.
3. Cover a roasting pan or cast-iron pan with foil.
4. Pat the chicken dry and brush the skin with olive oil.
5. Mix spices in a small bowl and rub spices over the chicken.
6. Open a beer or ginger ale can, pour half of it into the roasting pan, and stick the can inside the chicken. Set the chicken upright on the roasting pan with a chicken stand. In a pinch, use an empty vegetable can or Bundt pan.
7. Pour another 12 oz. of beer or ginger ale into the bottom of the roasting pan.
8. Place in oven and cook for 20 minutes per pound of chicken and until the thickest part of the meat reaches an internal temperature of 180°F.
9. Remove from oven, cover with foil, and rest for 10 minutes before serving.

Oven Roasted Chicken Quarters

Temp: 425°F   **Cook Time:** 40 min.

Ingredients:

- 6-8 chicken leg quarters
- 2 tsp dried basil
- 1 tsp salt
- 1 tsp garlic powder
- olive oil

Brine

- ⅓ cup salt
- 6 cups water

Instructions:

1. Brine chicken quarters for 2-6 hours in the refrigerator.
2. Preheat oven to 425°F.
3. Mix spices in a small bowl and set aside.
4. Remove chicken from brine, pat dry each chicken piece (including under the skin), and lay them on two oiled and foil-lined baking pans.
5. Brush oil on top of and underneath the chicken skin.
6. Pat seasoning underneath and on top of the chicken skin.
7. Place pans in oven for 40 minutes. The internal temperature in the thickest part of the meat should be 170°F and the skin crispy.
8. Remove from oven and serve.

Sweet and Sour Chicken

Temp: 350°F   **Cook Time:** 40 min.

Ingredients:

- 3-4 chicken breasts
- ½ tsp salt
- ½ tsp pepper
- ½ tsp paprika
- 1 cup cornstarch
- 2-3 eggs, beaten

Sauce

- ⅔ cup sugar
- ½ cup red wine vinegar
- ⅓ cup ketchup
- 1 tbl soy sauce
- 1 cup canned pineapple juice
- 2 tbls cornstarch
- 1 cup canned pineapple chunks

Brine

- ¼ cup salt
- 4 cups water

Instructions:

1. Brine chicken breasts for 4 hours in the refrigerator.
2. Preheat oven to 350°F.
3. Fill a shallow dish with cornstarch and another with the beaten eggs.
4. Dip chicken in cornstarch, egg, then cornstarch again.
5. Bring a thin layer of olive oil to a medium-high heat in a large, oven-safe fry pan.
6. Add chicken to the pan and fry on all sides for about 10 minutes total. Put the pan in the oven for 15 minutes.
7. Whisk sauce ingredients except the pineapple chunks in a medium saucepan, bringing it to a low boil until thick. Add pineapple chunks to the sauce.
8. Pull chicken out of the oven and pour sauce over the chicken.
9. Return to oven for 5-10 minutes. Serve with fried rice.

Henry

One could not have found a more hardworking nine-year-old delivering papers in the whole city. Or a cuter one. Granted, I looked like some ruffian out of a Dicken's novel, but I was cute, nonetheless. Oversized pants, probably my brother's shirt, well-loved sneakers, and a baseball cap that didn't do much to hide my fine, blonde hair. I think most people thought I was a homeless little urchin just trying to make a buck. In reality, I was just very industrious. I loved to work. So, what better job to have than delivering papers?

And yet, there was more to this job than just making money. At some point, I won a contest, and the prize was a turkey. Not a frozen turkey, no. A real, live turkey. My dad was unconvinced that I actually won the contest (at nine years old, I wasn't exactly the top worker on the route). "I doubt you won it," he said. "Nobody wanted to take it home, more like." But I did.

He was beautiful. And so much fun. We became best buds, me and that turkey. Granted, I had a lot of pets, being the baby of the family. Most of them hardly belonged in the midst of suburbia. This turkey was no different. But he was mine, and I called him Henry.

But Henry was not the best-behaved turkey. Besides digging in the garden, which my dad prized, and waking everyone up at ungodly hours, Henry had a bad habit of getting into the neighbor's yard to terrorize their dog. Or perhaps to be terrorized. The dog always ended up chasing Henry back over the fence, but that did not stop him. Henry was incorrigible. I regularly had to chase him back to our yard when I got home.

But one day, after maybe a week or so, Henry didn't come home. There was not much to be said about this. As I mentioned before, I had a great number of pets, and they came and went. Unfortunately, I also had an older brother. Worse, Thanksgiving was around the corner. And what did we have for dinner on Thanksgiving?

"How does Henry taste?" my brother teased during dinner.

My tears were profuse, my sobs unceasing. I was eating my beloved pet. And my brother found it hilarious.

"Stop teasing your sister," my dad scolded. "This isn't her turkey."

Now, I don't actually know if I ate Henry that night. I probably will never know what actually happened to my beloved pet. Did he end up on our holiday table? Did he join his turkey friends in the woods? Did another young girl adopt him as her treasured pet? I don't know. But today I keep turkeys, both as pets and for food. So, wherever he ended up, it was as it should be.

Baked Italian Meatballs

Temp: 375°   **Cook Time:** 15 min.

Ingredients:

- 1 cup parmesan cheese, grated
- ⅔ cup panko crumbs
- 2 tsp garlic powder
- 1 tsp dried oregano
- 1 tbl dried basil
- 2 tsp salt
- 2 lbs. lean ground turkey
- 2 eggs, beaten
- 3 tbls olive oil

Instructions:

1. In a small bowl, mix parmesan, breadcrumbs, and spices.
2. In a large bowl, break apart the ground turkey. Add in the spice mixture.
3. Beat the eggs in a small bowl and add to the meat mixture and combine everything thoroughly.
4. Preheat oven to 375° and line a baking sheet with foil and coat with pan spray.
5. Scoop out meat to form 1 ½" balls (or desired size).
6. Place meatballs on the foil-covered baking sheet and brush with olive oil.
7. Bake meatballs in the oven for 15 minutes or until they reach an internal temperature of 165°F.
8. Add to your desired dish or cool and freeze.

Swedish Meatballs

Cook Time: 40 min.

Ingredients:

Meatballs

- 1 ½ lbs. ground beef
- 3 slices white bread, crumbled
- 1 ½ tbls parsley
- ¾ tsp ground nutmeg
- ¾ tsp garlic powder
- 1 ½ tsp salt
- 1 ½ eggs

- olive oil

Sauce

- 3 tbls butter
- 3 tbls flour
- 2 cups beef broth
- 1 cup heavy cream
- ½ tbl Worcestershire sauce
- ½ tsp garlic powder
- ¼ tsp salt

- 1 lb. egg noodles

Instructions:

1. Combine meatball ingredients from ground beef to eggs in a large bowl.
2. Roll into meat mixture into 30 small, 2 tbls meatballs.
3. In a large fry pan, cook meatballs in olive oil at a medium heat until they are browned and cooked throughout.
4. In a medium saucepan, whisk butter and flour for the sauce at a medium heat for 2 minutes.
5. Whisk in broth, heavy cream, and Worcestershire sauce. Bring to a simmer.
6. Once the sauce begins to thicken, remove from heat and add salt and pepper.
7. Boil egg noodles until they are tender.
8. Drain noodles and add meatballs and sauce to serve.

Sweet and Sour Meatballs

Cook Time: 30 min.

Ingredients:

- 1 ½ cups basmati rice
- 3 cups water
- 2 tbls olive oil

Meatballs

- 1 ½ lbs. lean ground meat
- 1 cup breadcrumbs (2 slices white bread)
- 1 egg
- 1 tsp salt

- olive oil

Sauce

- 2 tbls cornstarch
- ½ cup brown sugar
- 1 cup pineapple juice
- ½ cup ketchup
- ¼ cup apple cider vinegar
- 1 tbl barbeque sauce

Instructions:

1. Bring water to a boil in a medium saucepan, add rice, and cover and boil for 15-20 minutes until water is absorbed.
2. Turn off heat and stir in olive oil.
3. Mix ground meat, breadcrumbs, egg, and salt in a large bowl.
4. Shape meat into twenty-four balls and brown in a fry pan (with olive oil if not using beef) until entirely cooked.
5. In a medium bowl, mix the sauce ingredients.
6. Drain grease from meatballs and pour sauce over them.
7. Simmer on low for 5 minutes to thicken the sauce.
8. Remove from heat and serve meatballs and sauce over rice.

Meatloaf

Temp: LOW, or 350°F   **Cook Time:** 5 hrs., or 55 min.

Ingredients:

- 1 lb. ground beef
- 1 lb. ground pork
- ⅓ cup ketchup
- 2 tbls brown sugar
- 1 ½ tbls garlic, minced
- ½ cup parmesan cheese, grated
- 2 eggs, beaten
- ½ tsp parsley flakes
- ½ tsp dried oregano
- 1 tsp salt
- 1 tsp onion powder
- ¾ cup panko crumbs, breadcrumbs, or ground oatmeal

Glaze

- ¼ cup brown sugar
- 1 cup ketchup

Instructions:

1. Thoroughly combine meats with ketchup and brown sugar.
2. Add the remaining ingredients from parmesan to breadcrumbs and combine well.
3. Line a large crockpot with foil or grease two 9x5" bread pans.
4. Form meat into a loaf shape in the crockpot or pans
5. Mix brown sugar and ketchup in a small dish and evenly coat the top of the meatloaf with glaze.
6. Cook in the crockpot on LOW for 5 hours or in preheated oven at 350°F for 55 minutes.
7. Internal temperature should reach 165°F.
8. Remove from dishes, slice, and serve.

Shepherd's Pie

Temp: 400°F   **Cook Time:** 25 min.

Ingredients:

- 1 lb. lean ground meat
- ¼ cup garlic, minced
- 1 tsp parsley
- 1 tsp salt
- ½ tsp pepper
- 2 tbls ketchup
- 1 tsp cornstarch
- ½ cup broth
- 1 cup corn
- 1 cup peas

- ½ cup carrots, diced
- 2 tbls butter
- 4 cups potatoes, diced
- 2 oz. cream cheese
- ¼ cup butter
- ⅓ cup milk
- 1 tsp salt
- ¾ cup cheddar cheese, shredded

Instructions:

1. Brown ground meat in a medium fry pan. Drain grease into a safe container and return meat to the pan with garlic, parsley, salt, pepper, and ketchup. Stir for 5 minutes on low heat.
2. Spread the meat mixture evenly into a 9x13" baking dish.
3. Preheat oven to 400°F.
4. Whisk cornstarch and broth in the pan and add vegetables and butter. Stir for 5 minutes and then add to the meat.
5. Bring 6 cups of water to a boil.
6. Peel, dice, and boil potatoes until tender and then drain.
7. Beat potatoes with cream cheese, butter, milk, and salt until they are fluffy. Spread evenly across vegetables.
8. Sprinkle cheese evenly across the potatoes and place the dish in the oven for 25 minutes.
9. Remove from oven, cool for 10-15 minutes, and serve.

Pork Chops

Temp: 350°F   **Cook Time:** 35 min.

Ingredients:

- ½ cup parmesan cheese, grated
- ½ cup panko crumbs
- 1 tsp dried basil
- ¼ tsp salt
- 4 large pork chops
- 4 tbls butter
- 4 tbls olive oil

Brine

- 4 tbls salt
- 6 cups water

Instructions:

1. Brine pork chops for a minimum of 3 hours in the refrigerator.
2. Heat two large cast-iron or oven-safe pans to medium-high on the stove with olive oil and butter.
3. Preheat oven to 350°F.
4. Mix parmesan cheese and panko crumbs in a wide and shallow bowl.
5. Coat pork chops evenly with parmesan mixture.
6. Sear pork chops in the cast iron for 3-5 minutes on each side.
7. Turn off the heat, cover the cast-iron pans with foil, and place it in the oven for 25 minutes.
8. The internal temperature of pork chops should be at least 165°F.
9. Remove from oven, remove foil, and serve.

Pork Roast

Temp: 325°F   **Cook Time:** 2 ½ hrs.

Ingredients:

- 4-5 lbs. boneless pork loin
- 2 tsp salt
- 2 tsp garlic powder
- 1 tbl flour
- 6 tbls butter
- ½ cup applesauce

Instructions:

1. Preheat oven to 325°F.
2. Mix salt, garlic, and flour in a small bowl and rub on the pork.
3. Sear pork in butter in an oven-safe pan.
4. Cover pork and pan with foil and cook in the oven for 1 ½ hours.
5. Top pork with the applesauce, tent with foil, and return to oven for another 30 minutes and until internal temperature reaches 160°F.
6. Remove from oven, slice, and serve.

Pork Schnitzel

Cook Time: 30 min.

Ingredients:

- 2 lbs. boneless pork chops
- ½ cup flour
- 1 tbl garlic salt
- ½ tsp paprika
- ½ tsp black pepper, freshly ground
- 2 eggs, beaten
- 1 cup panko crumbs
- olive oil

Dill Sauce
- 2 tbls flour
- 1 ½ cups chicken broth
- 1 cup sour cream
- ½ tsp dill weed

Instructions:

1. Trim pork chops of fat and slice into ½" thick cutlets.
2. Lightly pound to thin and tenderize.
3. Set up three bowls. In the first combine flour, garlic salt, paprika, and pepper. In the second, beat 2 eggs. In the third bowl, add the panko crumbs.
4. Dredge both sides of each cutlet in flour, then dip in beaten egg, then bread in panko crumbs.
5. Once the cutlets are breaded, heat a large fry pan to a medium heat and coat the bottom of the pan with olive oil.
6. Once the oil is hot, sauté cutlets for 3-4 minutes per side or until cooked and juices run clear. Set pork in a warm place.
7. Whisk flour and broth for dill sauce in a small bowl.
8. Add to the pan and bring to a boil, stirring constantly. Cook and stir for 2 minutes or until thickened.
9. Reduce heat to low and stir in sour cream and dill.
10. Once warmed, serve with pork.

Pulled Pork

Temp: LOW   **Cook Time:** 8 hrs.

Ingredients:

- 1 cup chicken broth
- ¼ cup apple cider vinegar
- ¼ cup brown sugar
- 3 tbls garlic, minced
- 4 lbs. pork loin
- 2 tsp salt
- 1 tbl Worcestershire sauce
- 1 cup barbeque sauce

Instructions:

1. In a large crock pot, mix broth, vinegar, brown sugar, and garlic.
2. Set the pork in a crock pot and rub it with salt and Worcestershire sauce.
3. Cover and cook on LOW for 8 hours. Internal temperature should reach 190°F for ideal tenderness but should be at a minimum of 160°F.
4. Remove two cups of the juice before shredding. This can be returned, but too much juice will water down the barbeque sauce.
5. Shred pork with forks, mix with remaining juices and barbeque sauce, and serve.

Of Cabbages and Kings

Brassicas are among the less-than-pleasant-smelling group of vegetables. They are like something between rotten eggs and seaweed. And yet, as a member of a Polish family, I have come not only to tolerate the smell but also enjoy the taste of a couple of members of this species, even cabbage. Stuffed Cabbages, or gołąbki, were a staple growing up. But until recently, I could never get past the smell. Even now, the smell of any member of the brassica family brings me back to many days of my childhood. Their smells are distinct. Brussels sprouts remind me of my dad's parents and having dinner at their house. Broccoli brings me back to one fateful night at the dinner table when our protein was more than the pork. And cabbage reminds me of crockpot dinners when I was a child and we were constantly going back and forth to the hospital, trips that brought smells of their own.

I am not sure about you, but for me, smells never really go away, not in memory. One breath, and a flood of moments return. Some are good, and some are bad. Any time I enter a hospital, I am once again a nine-year-old watching over her two younger brothers in a waiting room, waiting for my mom and grandpa to return. Or I am sitting in a car, hearing a machine remove the contents of my grandfather's lungs so he can breathe, and sitting in the car for an hour before those contents with their smell could be removed. I could not describe it to you — nor do you or I want me to — but it is there all the same.

Not exactly appetizing, I know. But those memories stay with me. When I think of certain foods, they remind me of certain people. Polish foods especially remind me of my grandpa, who I hardly got to know. And my last memories of him are associated with hospital smells, wet coughs, and little ability to eat.

But those memories were not all bad, smells and all. I can remember one of those afternoons with my grandpa in the van. My mom had helped him with his machine while sitting in front of a dollar store (back when things were still a dollar). All five of us — my mom, grandpa, me, and my two younger brothers — had just left that store. My grandpa (yes, the one with the lung problem) needed a pack of cigarettes, another smell I can pick out in moments, even when people try to hide it.

We were about to leave when my mom remembered she had to go back and grab something. When she returned, we watched as a man stopped her, asking for money. She gave him something and then returned to the car. My grandpa turned to her.

"How much did you give to him?"

My mom shrugged, "A $10."

He reached into his back pocket, pulled out his wallet, and tossed my mom a $20.

"The Lord returns double," he said. And we drove him home.

I am not sure that is in the Bible, exactly. But my grandpa was like that: generous and quick-witted. I laugh every time I think of that moment. I think of it every time I get a hint of that smell that permeated our car most days when I was nine. And for some reason, the smell of boiled cabbage reminds me of him. Perhaps it's because the smell has a sour aspect to it, or because it's willing to wrap up anything and make it into a new dish. My grandpa was creative like that, and so I think of him and my mom when I make stuffed cabbages.

My grandpa could not eat things like cabbage by then. Soon, he would not be able to eat, or say, anything at all. But stuffed cabbages were a favorite in my house at that time, that time when we spent all day away from home with my grandpa. Stuffed cabbages were easy, could be left all day, and you would know exactly what you were having when you walked in the door that evening. And like my grandpa, stuffed cabbages like to give back double in the form of leftovers, providing a hearty meal for days to come.

Gołąbki (Stuffed Cabbage)

Temp: 350°F   **Cook Time:** 1 ½ hrs.

Ingredients:

- 1 head of cabbage (about 3 lbs.)
- ½ cup breadcrumbs or rice
- ½ cup broth, hot
- 1 tbl olive oil
- 2 tbls garlic, minced
- 2 lbs. lean ground meat

- 2 eggs, beaten
- 6 oz. tomato puree
- 1 tbl parsley flakes
- 1 ½ tsp salt
- ¼ tsp pepper
- 28 oz. crushed tomatoes
- 8 oz. tomato sauce
- 2 tbls sugar

Instructions:

1. Bring a large stock pot of salted water to a boil, enough that your cabbage will be covered once it is in the pot.
2. Core the cabbage and place it core side down into the water and simmer for 10 minutes. Remove and cool.
3. Preheat oven to 350°F.
4. Combine breadcrumbs, broth, olive oil, garlic, meat, eggs, tomato puree, and spices in a large bowl. Alternatively, boil rice in the broth.
5. Set the largest cabbage leaves on a clean surface.
6. Spoon ¼-½ cup of the meat into the center of the leaves.
7. Roll and tuck leaves around the meat tightly.
8. Place rolls seam side down into a 9x13" baking dish.
9. Mix the crushed tomatoes, tomato sauce, and sugar in a medium bowl and pour over the rolls.
10. Cover with foil and cook in the oven for 1 ½ hours.
11. Serve hot, or cool and freeze for later.

Crockpot Unstuffed Cabbage

Temp: HIGH   **Cook Time:** 4-5 hrs.

Ingredients:

- 1 cup rice
- 2 cups broth
- ½ lb. bacon, chopped
- 2 lbs. ground beef
- 1 lb. ground pork
- 2 eggs, beaten
- 16 oz. tomato sauce
- 4 cloves garlic, minced
- 2 tsp salt
- 1 tsp pepper
- ½ tsp garlic powder
- ¼ tsp smoked paprika
- 1 onion, diced
- 1 medium head of cabbage, chopped
- 1 qt. crushed tomatoes
- 2 cups diced tomatoes
- 1 cup water

Instructions:

1. Boil rice in broth. Set aside.
2. Fry bacon in a medium frypan. Set it aside.
3. Sweat onions in bacon grease.
4. Combine ground beef and pork in a large bowl.
5. Add rice, bacon, onion, eggs, tomato sauce, garlic, and spices, and combine well.
6. Wash and chop up the cabbage.
7. Layer the following in a large crock pot: ½ of the crushed tomatoes, ⅓ of the chopped cabbage, ½ of the meat, ⅓ of the cabbage, remaining meat, remaining cabbage, diced tomatoes, and remaining crushed tomatoes.
8. Pour 1 cup of water over the top.
9. Cover the crock pot and cook on HIGH for 4-5 hours.

Barbecue Ribs

Temp: 300°F   **Cook Time:** 3 hrs. 40 min.

Ingredients:

- 1 slab bone-in pork ribs
- 4 cups water
- 2 tbls sugar
- 2 tbls salt
- BBQ sauce (p. 165)
- brown sugar
- rib seasoning

Instructions:

1. In a large bowl with a lid, dissolve sugar and salt in water. Marinate ribs for 3-24 hours.
2. Preheat oven to 300°F.
3. Lay two sheets of foil on a baking pan and set on the counter.
4. Set the ribs on a few sheets of paper towel. Remove the rib membrane by taking a butter knife and sliding it underneath the membrane at a bone a third of the way up the rib. Pull off with a piece of paper towel.
5. Pat ribs dry and set on the foil.
6. Pat ribs with a dry rub, such as brown sugar or other seasonings, and then cover in most of the sauce.
7. Flip ribs upside down and wrap them with the first layer of foil, then flip back and wrap them with the second layer.
8. Cook ribs for 3 ½ hours.
9. Remove ribs from the oven, open the foil (but leave ribs on the foil) and brush with remaining sauce. If you have no sauce ribs, add a bit more brown sugar and butter.
10. Put ribs back in the oven for 10 minutes and broil so the sauce caramelizes. This can also be done on a grill.
11. Remove from oven and serve.

Beer Brats

Cook Time: 20 min.

Ingredients:

- 4 bratwursts
- 4 tbls butter
- 1 tbl garlic, minced
- 1 cup dark ale, beer, or ginger ale

Instructions:

1. Heat a 10" cast-iron pan to a medium-high.
2. Add the butter and heat until it begins to brown.
3. Sear bratwurst for about 2-3 minutes per side for a nice golden brown, not burned.
4. Add garlic and ale or beer and bring to a boil.
5. Once you have reached a boil, turn the heat to low. Continue cooking and turning brats for 10-15 minutes. If these are fresh, be sure that the internal temperature reaches 165°F.
6. Let the liquid reduce and then remove and serve.
   a. Alternatively, after step 3, add everything to a crock pot and cook on MEDIUM for 4 hours.

Pot Roast

Temp: LOW

Cook Time: 8 hrs.

Ingredients:

- 2 tbls flour
- 2 tsp salt
- 2 tsp garlic powder
- 2 tsp onion powder
- 1 tbl Worcestershire sauce
- 3 lbs. chuck roast
- 2 tbls olive oil

- 4 medium potatoes, quartered
- ½ lb. baby carrots
- ¼ cup yellow onion, sliced
- 2 cups beef broth
- 1 tbl garlic, diced
- 4 tbls butter

Instructions:

1. Combine flour with spices. Rub Worcestershire sauce and spice mixture over roast.
2. Sear roast in olive oil for 4 minutes per side in a cast-iron pan.
3. Set washed and quartered potatoes, baby carrots, and sliced onions in a large crockpot.
4. Add broth and garlic to the vegetables.
5. Set the roast on top of the vegetables and pour the juices in the pan over the roast and top with butter.
6. Cover and cook on LOW for 8 hours. Internal temperature should reach 195°F for ideal tenderness but should be at a minimum of 160°F.
7. Remove from the crockpot, slice, and serve.

The Biggest Catch

Happy gurgling met the ears of the three fishers on the side of the bank. Father, son, and daughter. The Detroit River was as close to peace on earth, and certainly as close to Pennsylvania, as any of them would be getting for the foreseeable future. Smoke trailed lazily around the face of the children's father, and both of their heads moved eagerly with each dip of the bobber. From time to time, a fish would jump to catch a fly, pleasantly disturbing the gentle flow of the river. Nothing was imperfect on a summer day fishing.

The father looked over at his two children. Their eyes were on the water, expecting a fish at any moment, but his eyes were on them. Was this what it was like for his father on the rare days they went fishing behind their house in Wilkes-Barre? Did his father eagerly await those afternoons as he now did? He turned back to the river, frowning in contemplation. No fish tugged on his line, but they didn't always. It was the patient, quiet wait that was half the joy. Even with the intermittent chatter, it was nice to have company. Even if they scared away the fish, it was nice to have them near.

His son's bobber went down, and he jumped up. "Dad, I think I got one!" His son's feet skittered with excitement, and he nearly dropped his pole.

"Ok, let's reel 'em in slowly." He could see it was a small fish, but it was big enough for a cheer from his daughter and the nervous dance of his son.

"Slowly now. We don't want 'em breaking free." He stood behind his son, guiding his hand on the reel, letting the fish hook himself further and further. They could see his quick fins below the surface of the green water, his scales shimmering between his splashes in the sun. Their father got the net, and together they brought the fish in.

"It's a bluegill, Dad!" His son shouted as if he had never seen the fish before. Their father smiled.

"Wow, look at his spikes! Can I hold him?" his daughter inquired of her brother. He held out the fish to her, and she nearly dropped him. They laughed, and she quickly threw him in the bucket.

They returned to their lines. It was not long before his daughter caught a fish as well. She wanted no help reeling the small fry in, and she proudly held up her prize as he flipped his tail in the sun, showing off his greens, yellows, and blue.

"Can I keep him?" she looked up with pleading eyes.

"Sure, put 'em in the bucket." He would need to go back to the river, but she didn't need to know that.

His daughter carefully removed the hook from the fish's mouth, plopped him in the bucket, and got a new worm. Soon, the peace of the river returned, interrupted only by the call of a robin or blue jay. While they waited, the two snacked on pop, apple pies, and Twinkies.

Suddenly, his son jumped up again, excitement across his face. "Dad, I think I got another one! He's huge this time!" He wrestled with his line, knowing that this was going to be the catch of the day! Before their father could stand, the pole jerked back, freeing itself from the tangle of lake weed in a spray of water and muck, zipping through the air, and landing behind where they were sitting. Frustrated, he snapped the hook back towards the water, and through his sister's ear.

It was a worthy scream, made worthier by the laughter of her brother and father to follow. But their mirth was short-lived. Together, the three of them trudged back to their picnic table to gather the remaining party store snacks and their father's tackle box.

"Sorry, Joey," her brother said, trying to hide his smile. "It really was an accident."

Tears streaming down her face, she stuck her tongue out at him and climbed into the car. Chuckling, her father responded, "Really, Joey, this is a win-win. You did want to get your ears pierced, after all!" Father and son laughed together, and a smile might have made an appearance on the aggrieved party's face as well.

Providentially, the hospital was just behind them, so it didn't take long before they were waiting with others to be seen for various ailments. Soon they met the doctor, and he was less than amused by the situation. But his sympathy ended there. "No worries," he lied, "this will numb the pain." But her ear was not numb as the doctor cut the hook in half and removed it from her pierced ear.

As they reached the car, their father patted her shoulder. "How are you feeling?" he asked.

"Miserable." She wiped a tear from her face.

"Well, I guess that means we should head home!"

"No!" She shook her head, tears vanishing from her face. "I want to catch one more fish!" And she bolted back toward the river, fishing pole in hand. Her father smiled, watching her blonde hair dance as she plopped onto the edge of the riverbank. Together, her father and brother joined her to fish out the rest of the afternoon summer sun. This was peace. This was heaven. Nothing could ruin a day such as this.

Fajitas

Cook Time: 15 min.

Ingredients:

- 1 lb. chicken breasts or tenders, sliced
- ½ tsp salt
- ½ tsp pepper
- ½ tsp chili powder
- 1 tsp ground cumin
- 1 tbl garlic, minced
- olive oil
- 1 medium green pepper
- 1 medium red pepper
- 1 small yellow onion
- 1 ½ cups Mexican cheese, shredded
- sour cream
- tortillas

Instructions:

1. Slice chicken into thin 3" strips and place in a large bowl. Mix seasonings in a small bowl. Toss chicken with seasonings.
2. Add seasoned chicken to a medium fry pan with olive oil, cover the pan, and heat at medium-high for 5 minutes, or until it reaches an internal temperature of 165°F.
3. Slice peppers and onion into strips and add to fry pan with chicken. Sauté for 5 minutes.
4. Add to tortillas with cheese and sour cream and serve.

Hawaiian Ham and Cheese

Temp: 350°F   **Cook Time:** 30 min.

Ingredients:

- 12 Hawaiian rolls
- 3 tbls butter, melted
- 1 tbl Dijon mustard
- 1 tbl honey
- 1 lb. sliced ham
- ½ lb. Swiss cheese, sliced or shredded
- ½ lb. cheddar cheese, sliced or shredded

Instructions:

1. Preheat oven to oven to 350°F.
2. In a small bowl, mix butter, mustard, and honey.
3. Line a 9x13" pan with foil.
4. Slice rolls in half so you have two slabs of rolls.
5. Brush bottom of bottom half lightly with the butter mixture and place in the pan. Set the other half aside.
6. Alternate layers of ham and cheese across the rolls until you have used up everything.
7. Add the top half of the rolls onto the meat and cheese and brush the rolls with the remaining butter mixture.
8. Cover with foil and bake for 20 minutes.
9. Remove foil and bake for an additional 10 minutes.
10. Remove from oven, cut, and serve.

Mini Pizza Rolls

Cook Time: 30 min.

Ingredients:

- 12 oz. package square wonton wrappers

  Or
    - 2 cups flour
    - 1 tsp salt
    - 1 egg
    - ½ cup water
    - cornstarch
- olive or canola oil
- 2 cups mozzarella cheese, shredded
- ¾ cup pizza sauce
- 1 cup pepperoni, chopped
- ½ tbl Italian seasoning
- parmesan cheese, grated

Instructions:

1. Stir together mozzarella cheese, pizza sauce, pepperoni, and Italian seasoning in a medium bowl.
2. To make the wonton wrappers:
    a. Mix flour, salt, egg, and water in a small bowl to form a soft, non-sticky dough. Knead for 5 minutes.
    b. Cover and rest for 30 minutes.
    c. Divide in two. Cover one half of the dough and roll out the other to no more than ⅛" thick.
    d. Cut into 4" squares and dust with cornstarch. Repeat with all the dough.
3. Spoon ½ tbl of filling into the center of each wonton wrapper. Wet, fold, and seal the edges.
4. Heat 2" of oil in a saucepan to 350°F and fry the rolls until they are golden. This should take 2 minutes per side.
5. Remove from oil and drain on a piece of paper towel.
6. Sprinkle parmesan on top before fully dry, cool, and serve.

Pasties

Temp: 375°F

Cook Time: 50-60 min.

Ingredients:

Crust
- 1 cup butter, cold
- 3 ½ cups flour
- 1 tsp salt
- 1 egg, beaten
- 7-8 tbls water
- 2 tsp white or apple cider vinegar

Filling
- 1 cup carrots, diced
- 2 cups potatoes, diced
- ½ cup yellow onion, diced
- 1 lb. 4 oz. lean ground meat
- 1 tbl garlic, minced
- 1 tbl parsley flakes
- 2 tsp salt
- 1 ½ tsp pepper
- 1 egg, beaten
- 6 tbls butter, cold
- 1 egg, beaten

Instructions:

1. Cut butter into flour and salt. Mix in egg, water, and vinegar. Form into a dough. Wrap and refrigerate for 15 minutes.
2. Peel, wash, and dice carrots, potatoes, and onion. Add to a large bowl and combine with meat, spices, and egg.
3. Preheat oven to 375°F.
4. Divide dough into 6 pieces and roll into 8" circles.
5. Scoop 1 cup of filling into each dough circle. Top with butter.
6. Fold the dough over into a semi-circle. Fold and crimp the edges to seal the pasty.
7. Brush dough with beaten egg.
8. Cut slits into the top of the dough and bake in the oven for 50-60 minutes, or until the crust is golden.

Sloppy Joes

Cook Time: 20 min.

Ingredients:

- 2 lbs. lean ground beef
- ⅔ green pepper, diced
- 1 medium onion, diced
- 4 cloves garlic, minced
- 1 ½ cups ketchup
- 2 tbls yellow mustard
- 2 tbls brown sugar
- 8-10 hamburger buns

Instructions:

1. Brown ground beef in a large fry pan. Drain grease into a safe container.
2. Add peppers, onion, and garlic and sauté until tender.
3. Add the remaining ingredients and simmer for 5 minutes.
4. Remove from heat and serve on hamburger buns.

Who Dunnit?

Joey and Steve could smell the simmering sauce before they opened the front door. Smiles lit both of their faces. They could practically see the bubbling tomatoes, the boiling noodles, and the perfectly seasoned beef. But as they stepped inside, they paused.

Whose spaghetti was this?

They tapped down their enthusiasm for a moment, wondering if they should enter the kitchen first or put away their books. After all, what would they find in that pot? Would it be the smooth, delicious, warm-your-heart meat sauce that Dad made, or would it be the clumpy, greasy, make-you-want-to-gag sauce that Mom made?

Curious, the two smelled the air again, but they could not discern the appeal from scent alone, not with every other flavor that filled the room, a mix of cheap perfume and cigarette ash. They took a nervous step forward and chose their rooms instead. As they passed the kitchen, they took a quick look inside. There was no sign of either parent in the kitchen, but that didn't mean much. Either could have been anywhere in the house, even with the stove on.

With haste, they dropped their books in their rooms and hurried back to the kitchen. The pot was covered, the bubbling reached their ears, and the noodles were nearly ready. Steve lifted the lid slightly, and Joey looked inside. A sigh, and a smile. Dad made this spaghetti. Joey's stomach rumbled, and together the two of them got their plates, quickly filling them with the perfect, savory meal.

Silence settled between the two as they sat down at the table to eat their dinner, careful to clear a space on the overcrowded surface. Focusing on the meal in front of them, it was a few minutes before they realized what day tomorrow was: Saturday. As though sharing the same thought, they looked up and smiled, then returned to the feast before them. Tomorrow they would wake up to the same dish, but with a topping of scrambled eggs — Dad's unique cuisine.

Slow, heavy steps made their way up the stairs. Joey looked up and Steve turned around as they watched their dad pause in the doorframe to the basement. He nodded with a grunt and moved towards the stove to make his own plate. Sitting down with his two youngest, he finished dinner with them quietly, perhaps contemplating today, perhaps looking forward to the morning when there would be no questions of who made what or what there was to be. There would only be what there always had been after an evening like tonight: spaghetti and eggs made by Dad, and fleeting moments of family.

Baked Mostaccioli

Temp: 350°F   **Cook Time:** 30 min.

Ingredients:

- 1 ½ lbs. lean ground meat
- 1 lb. penne pasta
- 1 tsp dried oregano
- 2 tbls garlic, minced
- 3 ½ cups pasta sauce
- 1 ½ cups mozzarella cheese, shredded
- ½ cup parmesan cheese, grated

Instructions:

1. Preheat oven to 350°F.
2. Bring a large pot of water to a boil.
3. Brown ground meat in a medium fry pan. Drain grease if necessary.
4. Stir in oregano and garlic into ground meat.
5. Boil penne pasta al dente.
6. Drain pasta and pour into a 9x13" baking dish.
7. Mix in meat, sauce, and half of the parmesan.
8. Top with mozzarella and the remainder of the parmesan.
9. Cook for 30 minutes until the cheese is barely golden.
10. Remove from oven and serve.

Beef Stroganoff

Cook Time: 35 min.

Ingredients:

- 16 oz. egg noodles
- 1 ½ lbs. sirloin steak
- 3 tbls flour
- ½ tsp salt
- ¼ tsp pepper
- 2 tbls olive oil
- 3 tbls butter
- 2 tbls garlic, minced
- 2 cups broth
- 2 tsp Worcestershire sauce
- ½ cup sour cream
- ½ tbl parsley flakes

Instructions:

1. Bring a large pot of water to a boil and boil noodles until they are tender. Drain and set aside in a large serving bowl.
2. While the pasta boils, sear the steak in butter in a medium fry pan. Cook each side for 3 minutes at a time until fully cooked.
3. Remove and slice into bite-sized pieces. Set it aside.
4. Add garlic and spices to the pan.
5. In a small bowl, whisk together flour, Worcestershire sauce, and broth. Pour into pan and simmer for 5 minutes, stirring regularly.
6. Stir in sour cream and steak pieces.
7. Pour meat sauce over noodles, top with parsley, and serve.

Hamburger Mac and Cheese

Cook Time: 30 min.

Ingredients:

- 3 cups broth
- 16 oz. (2 cups) macaroni noodles
- 1 lb. ground beef
- 1 tbl butter
- 2 tbls ketchup
- 1 tsp garlic powder
- ½ tsp salt
- ⅛ tsp paprika

- 6 tbls butter
- 3 tbls flour
- 1 ½ cups milk
- ½ tsp salt
- 2 cups cheddar cheese, shredded

Instructions:

1. Bring broth to a boil in a large stock pot. Boil macaroni in the broth for about 8 minutes until all the liquid is absorbed. Once the liquid is absorbed, remove from heat.
2. While noodles boil, brown ground beef in a large fry pan.
3. Turn the heat to low and drain the grease from the meat.
4. Add butter, ketchup, and spices to ground beef. Stir together.
5. Add the meat to the noodles and stir together.
6. In a large saucepan, melt the butter and stir in flour. Continue stirring over a medium heat for 2 minutes.
7. Add milk and salt, turn up the heat, and whisk for about 2 minutes until it begins to thicken.
8. Add cheese. If the sauce is too thick, add more milk by the tablespoon.
9. Pour the cheese into the pot with macaroni and combine.
10. Serve with vegetable of choice.

Stovetop Mac and Cheese

Cook Time: 20 min.

Ingredients:

- 16 oz. (2 cups) macaroni noodles
- 6 cups water
- 6 tbls butter
- ⅓ cup flour
- ½ tsp salt
- ½ tsp garlic powder (optional)
- 1 tsp better than bullion paste (optional)
- 1 ¾ cups milk
- ¼ cup sour cream
- 2 cups cheddar cheese, shredded

Instructions:

1. Bring 6 cups of water to a boil in a large stock pot. Boil macaroni for 8-10 minutes until al dente. Do not overcook.
2. Drain noodles and set aside.
3. Reduce heat to medium and melt the butter in the stockpot. Stir in flour and seasonings. Continue stirring over a medium heat for 2 minutes.
4. Add 1 ½ cups milk and whisk for about 2 minutes until it begins to thicken.
5. Turn off heat and add macaroni, sour cream, and cheese to the stock pot, stirring until completely incorporated. If desired, add garlic powder and bullion paste. If needed, add remaining milk.
6. Serve with chopped meat or vegetable of choice.

Lasagna

Temp: 375°F   **Cook Time:** 40 min.

Ingredients:

- 8 cups meat pasta sauce (p. 162)
- 12 lasagna noodles
- olive oil
- 16 oz. ricotta cheese
- 1 ½ cups mozzarella cheese, shredded
- 2 tbls parsley flakes
- ½ tsp salt
- 1 egg, beaten
- 2 cups mozzarella cheese, shredded
- ½ cup parmesan cheese, grated

Instructions:

1. Prepare a meat pasta sauce (p. 162).
2. Boil noodles to al dente. Drain noodles, separate and coat with olive oil, and set aside.
3. Preheat oven to 375°F.
4. In a medium bowl, combine ricotta, 1 ½ cups mozzarella, parsley, salt, and egg.
5. Spread 1 ½ cups of the meat sauce in a 9x13" baking dish. Lay three noodles on top. Spread with ⅓ of ricotta mixture.
6. Repeat layering with remaining meat, noodles, and ricotta.
7. Top with mozzarella and parmesan.
8. Cover with foil and place in the oven for 30 minutes.
9. Remove foil and bake for another 10 minutes until the cheese is golden and bubbly.
10. Cool and serve.

Chili

Temp: MEDIUM   **Cook Time:** 4 hrs.

Ingredients:

- 1 ½ lbs. lean ground meat
- 30 oz. kidney beans, drained and rinsed
- 30 oz. black beans, drained and rinsed
- 28 oz. crushed tomatoes
- 6 oz. tomato paste
- 2 tbls garlic, minced
- 2 tsp chili powder
- 1 tsp ground cumin
- 1 tsp onion powder
- ¼ tsp cayenne pepper
- 1 tsp salt
- 12 oz. dark beer (optional)
- 1 cup broth (optional)
- shredded cheddar cheese
- sour cream

Instructions:

1. Brown ground meat in a medium frypan.
2. Drain if necessary and add to a large crock pot.
3. Drain and rinse beans and add to crock pot.
4. Stir in tomatoes, tomato paste, garlic, and spices.
5. Add dark beer or broth, if desired.
6. Turn the crockpot to MEDIUM and cook for 4 hours.
7. Top with cheese and sour cream.
8. Serve with cornbread or corn chips.

Chicken Chili

Cook Time: 1 hr.

Ingredients:

- 3 boneless chicken breasts
- 4 cups chicken broth
- 1 tsp chili powder
- 2 tsp ground cumin
- 1 tsp garlic powder
- 1 tsp dried oregano
- 1 tsp cayenne pepper
- 48 oz. white beans, drained and rinsed
- 4 oz. green chilies, diced
- 1 medium onion, diced
- 1 tsp Tabasco sauce
- Mexican cheese

Instructions:

1. In a large stock pot, boil chicken in chicken broth and chili powder for 30-40 minutes.
2. Once chicken is fully cooked, dice or shred chicken and add the remaining ingredients.
3. Simmer for 1 hour, top individual bowls with cheese, and serve.

There is a Season

Breathe in, breathe out. The day has come to a close. Behind you, the sun sets between the remaining leaves, highlighting their golden hues, and warming you with one more wink before saying, "Goodnight." The last patter of feet goes through the door, and you close it. Your oldest has already grabbed the sour cream and cheddar cheese, and the next is retrieving bowls and spoons. The youngest is sitting down munching on chips. He is the baby, after all. Breathe.

The smell of warmth, home, and tomatoes fills your nose. Yes, a dash of garlic, some bright spices, and the undertones of beans color your senses. This is a greeting to remember. This is a greeting filled with promise, with fullness, with rest. There were enough greetings today and almost as many goodbyes. But never enough. There is always room for one more embrace, one more farewell, one more. But tomorrow there will be another, and today there is chili and sleep.

Chatter greets you now as you move towards the table, and the spiciness is softened with a dash of cream and cheese. Yes, it is not how everyone does it, but it is how you do it, and now how they serve their own food. Warmth, family, home. There will be time for more care tomorrow, but now is a moment for rest as you listen to the voices surrounding you speaking of everything and nothing, something different from the day. For this is night, and the moon has said hello, twice for today. Breathe out, and it beckons you to sleep after such a stout meal.

Little blankets rise and fall with each passing moment, but you check on them one last time as you walk back to your room, tired, but fulfilled. This is only a time, but you only half realize it then. There will be times for laughter, embracing, and healing soon. And there will be times to be silent, to mourn, and to refrain. These times won't last. So, breathe, and rest. Tomorrow has enough of its own.

Soups

Bean with Ham Soup

Cook Time: 40 min.

Ingredients:

- 1 tbl butter
- 2 tbls garlic, minced
- 1 medium yellow onion, diced
- 1 ½ cups celery, diced
- 2 cups carrots, diced
- 1 tbl veggie pepper seasoning
- 1 qt. vegetable or beef broth
- 4 cups ham, diced
- (4) 15.5 oz. cans great northern beans, drained and rinsed

Instructions:

1. Sauté onion and garlic with butter in a medium fry pan at a medium-low heat until onions are translucent.
2. Dice celery and carrots and add to the onions.
3. Add seasoning and stir for 5 minutes.
4. Bring broth to a boil in a large stock pot.
5. Add vegetables and ham to the pot.
6. Drain and rinse beans and add to the pot.
7. Simmer for 30 minutes.
8. Using either an immersion blender or a large food processor, blend until the soup reaches desired consistency and serve.

Beef Barley Soup

Cook Time: 1 hr. 30 min.

Ingredients:

- 1 ½-2 lbs. beef chuck roast
- 2 tbls olive oil
- 2 tbls garlic, minced
- ½ tsp salt
- ½ tsp pepper
- 1 small yellow onion, diced
- 1 tbl Worcestershire sauce
- ⅓ cup Merlot wine
- 8 cups beef broth
- 28 oz. diced tomatoes
- 2 tbls tomato paste
- 1 ½ cups pearled or hulled barley
- 5 carrots, diced
- 2-3 celery stalks, diced

Instructions:

1. Chop beef into small pieces and add to a large Dutch oven with olive oil, garlic, salt, and pepper.
2. Brown beef at a medium-high heat for about 4 minutes.
3. Stir in onion, Worcestershire sauce, and red wine. Cook for another 2 minutes.
4. Add broth, tomatoes with juices, and tomato paste. Simmer covered for 15 minutes.
5. Add barley and simmer covered for an hour, or until barley is plump.
   a. Alternatively, cook in a crock pot for 8 hours on LOW.

Chicken and Bacon Gnocchi

Cook Time: 30 min.

Ingredients:

- 6 slices of bacon, chopped
- 2 chicken breasts
- 1 clove garlic, minced
- ½ cup chicken broth
- 1 cup heavy cream
- ¼ tsp Italian seasoning
- 1 lb. fresh potato gnocchi
- ½ cup parmesan cheese, grated
- ¼ tsp salt
- ¼ tsp pepper

Instructions:

1. Fry bacon in a large, deep fry pan until crispy.
2. Drain all but a tablespoon of grease from the pan.
3. Cook chicken breasts in a separate pan with some water and cover. Once the insides are no longer pink and the juices run clear, and the temperature reads 165°F, remove and chop.
4. Add the chicken to the hot bacon grease pan with the garlic.
5. Fry for a couple of minutes and add in the broth, cream, seasoning, bacon, and gnocchi and stir together.
6. Cover the pan and keep hot for 4 minutes.
7. Take off the lid and continue to cook until the liquid reduces to a thick sauce, stirring continually.
8. Add parmesan, salt, and pepper, and serve.

Chicken Soup for the Soul

The wind rattles the windows, sneaking drafts between the sills. Everyone was waiting for something to fill their bellies and hearts on this blustery day, something that made it feel a bit more like home and a little less like the dead of winter. The savory smell of sautéed onions fills the room along with the warm hint of the chicken stock boiling just minutes before. Together, they are inviting, calming, welcoming. Add a bit of pepper, some salt, and it is ready to join the stock. She adds chopped carrots for flavor and color, and some celery because that is how it is always done. She brings the boil to a low simmer, and the pot of soup is ready to sit a bit before the kluski noodles can be added. There is time yet, so she moves to the living room where she can still see and smell the soup, but rest a for a bit. It would be no good to leave a pot on a stove, let alone a gas one.

She can see it now. A few minutes to finish a little something, a few more to take care of something else, the liquid boiling down until all that is left are burnt onions and vegetables. But she would be outside by then, tending to one more item on her list before dinner is done. By then, the pan would get so hot that the vegetables catch fire, licking their way up the cabinets above the stove, creeping across the ceiling, making their way closer to the open window.

But no, this did not happen today, or even here. This happened years ago, one weekend long ago in May. Her dad stirred onions in the butter, and took a sip. He added the seasoning, and picked up the bottle once more. Did he add back the stock? Did he turn the heat up instead of down? Did he think of either of these things before laying down in his bedroom, not waking up to the flames or smoke but to their dog Guido, who was alerting the whole neighborhood with his cries? Afterward, all that was left was evidence of the flames. The blackened kitchen, the smoke-filled rooms, the burnt pot.

That would not happen here today, and that was not the last time her dad made soup. Though she was not there that day, and neither was anyone else, they would spend time in that kitchen again. He would show her how to stir ingredients to a savory flavor, filling the room with that warm aroma of home, cleansing their senses and minds of the smells and sights of a temporary hotel stay, of the scorched walls, of smoke made with just as much negligence as that which spilled from his mouth. But now, she thought not of that. Just of soup, and dinner, and adding the noodles to the pot, watching and boiling until they were just right.

The noodles! The pot had boiled down a bit by this point. Just a bit of water would make it right. Not too much to reduce the flavor, no, just enough for the noodles to drink up and leave more than a sip. She stirred the flavors together, blurring memories with each turn, and stopped. The smell of yeast begins to fill the kitchen now, and she removes a loaf of warm bread from the oven. Her dad would not have made this, but things can change. After all, nothing pairs with chicken soup like freshly made bread.

She calls up the stairs for the kids, but not before slicing off the heel for herself. A tumble of feet hurtles down the stairs, and now three hungry faces appear behind the back of the stove, ready for their bowls and bread. The four of them carefully bring their bowls to the table — the stove turned off — to sit together and talk and eat. This was home. The gathering of hungry mouths and close hearts, of warm spaces where distant traditions formed new memories with a simple meal.

Kluski Noodles

Ingredients:

- 1 ½-¾ cups flour
- 1 egg
- 2 egg yolks
- ½ tsp salt
- 1 tbls butter, melted
- 2-3 tbls water

Instructions:

1. Form a well with 1 ½ cups flour on the counter and add eggs, salt, and melted butter to the center.
2. Mix the wet ingredients in the center and then slowly incorporate the flour.
3. Once you have a crumbly texture, form the dough into a ball and knead for a couple of minutes until it has an elastic texture. You may need to add a splash of water or a bit of flour depending on if the dough is too dry or sticky.
4. Form the dough into ball and wrap it with plastic wrap to rest for 45 minutes. If you wish to make the noodles later, place the dough in a sealed container for up to 2 days.
5. Roll out the dough to ⅛" thick and cut into strips 4"-8" long and ¼"-¾" wide.
6. If you want to use noodles later, dry out the noodles to where they will not stick to each other and store them in a freezer bag or sealed container. They can be refrigerated for 4 days or frozen for 4 months.
7. Add noodles directly to your soup or bring a pot of salted water to a boil and add noodles, boiling for no more than 5 minutes. Drain and add to your dish.

Chicken Soup

Cook Time: 8 hrs.

Ingredients:

- 3-4 chicken leg quarters
- 1 gallon water
- 6 medium carrots
- 2 celery stalks
- 1 tsp dried basil
- ½ tsp pepper
- 2 tsp salt
- 2-3 tbls garlic, minced
- 2 tbls better than bouillon chicken paste
- 1 lb. egg noodles

Instructions:

1. Boil chicken quarters in the water in a large stock pot over 2 hours. You will need to regularly add more water. Alternatively, place quarters in a Dutch oven and simmer for 1 hour.
2. Remove chicken from the water and place in a bowl to cool. Once it has cooled, separate the bones from the meat.
3. Throw away any tiny bones and return the large bones, skin, and cartilage to the pot to boil for another 4-5 hours. Keep meat in the refrigerator.
4. Remove bones from the pot and add peeled and chopped carrots, diced celery, basil, pepper, salt, garlic, and bullion.
5. Simmer for 30 minutes.
6. Add chicken and noodles, simmer for another 8 minutes, and serve.

Cream of Broccoli

Cook Time: 45 min.

Ingredients:

- 5 tbls butter
- ⅓ cup yellow onion, minced
- 3 tbls flour
- 3 cups broth
- 1 cup milk
- 1 cup half and half
- 6 cups broccoli florets, chopped
- 1 tsp salt
- cheddar cheese, shredded (optional)

Instructions:

1. Sauté onion in butter in a medium stock pot for 5 minutes.
2. Whisk in flour and cook for another 2 minutes.
3. Either blend broccoli in a food processor now or use an immersion blender after step 5.
4. Add the broth, milk, cream, broccoli, and salt.
5. Simmer covered for 15 minutes.
6. Uncover the soup and continue simmering for another 10 minutes, stirring regularly, until the soup reaches the desired consistency.
7. If desired, serve with cheese.

Cream of Potato

Cook Time: 45 min.

Ingredients:

- 6 slices bacon
- ¼ cup yellow onion, diced
- 3 tbls flour
- 3 cups milk
- 2 cups broth
- 1 cup heavy cream
- 5 cups russet potatoes, diced
- 1 ½ tsp salt
- ¼ tsp pepper
- 1 cup cheddar cheese, shredded

Instructions:

1. Cook bacon in a large stock pot at a medium-low heat until it is crispy. Crumble and set the bacon aside on a paper towel. Leave grease in the pot.
2. Add the onion to the grease and sauté until translucent.
3. Stir in the flour and cook for 3 minutes.
4. Add the milk, broth, and cream.
5. Peel, wash, and dice the potatoes. Add the potatoes, salt, and pepper to the pot. Raise heat to medium and simmer for 15 minutes until the potatoes have softened.
6. Remove most of the potatoes with a slotted spoon and puree in a blender. This can also be done in-pot with an immersion blender. Then return the potatoes to the pot.
7. Turn off the heat, stir in cheese and bacon, and serve.

French Onion

Cook Time: 30 min.

Ingredients:

- ¼ cup butter
- 1 tbl brown sugar
- ½ tsp salt
- 1 tbl Worcestershire sauce
- 2 large yellow onions, quartered and sliced
- 4 cups beef broth
- 4 slices French bread
- 4 slices provolone cheese
- 4 tbls parmesan cheese, grated

Instructions:

1. In a large saucepan at a medium-low, melt butter and stir in brown sugar, salt, and Worcestershire sauce.
2. Add onions and sauté for 20 minutes.
3. Stir in broth and simmer for 20 minutes until onions are tender.
4. Ladle soup into 4 individual crocks and top with a slice of French bread, 1 tbl of parmesan cheese, and a slice of provolone cheese.
5. Set the crocks under the broiler for 4 minutes to melt the cheese.
6. Remove from oven and serve.

Kielbasa Soup

Cook Time: 35 min.

Ingredients:

- 4 tbls butter
- 1 medium yellow onion, diced
- 1 tbl garlic, minced
- ¼ cup flour
- 6 cups vegetable broth
- 1 cup half and half
- 2 stalks celery, diced
- 4 cups red potatoes, quartered
- 1 link smoked kielbasa, chopped
- ¼ cup kale, chopped
- 1 tbl spinach and herb seasoning

Instructions:

1. Sauté onion and garlic in butter until the onion is translucent.
2. Add flour and whisk for 3 minutes.
3. Add and whisk broth and half and half.
4. Add remaining ingredients and simmer for 20 minutes, or until potatoes are soft.
5. Remove from heat and serve.

Minestrone

Cook Time: 2 ½ hrs.

Ingredients:

- 6 slices of bacon
- 2 cloves garlic, minced
- 2 medium onions, diced
- 1 qt. tomatoes, diced
- 2 cups cabbage, diced
- 2 cups celery, diced
- 3 medium carrots, diced
- 2 potatoes, diced
- 1 cup zucchini, diced
- ¾ cup red pepper, diced
- 16 oz. kidney beans, drained and rinsed
- 16 oz. garbanzo beans, drained and rinsed
- 3 tbls parsley flakes
- ¼ tsp dried sage
- 1 tsp dried oregano
- 12 peppercorns
- 6 bay leaves
- 3 qts. water
- 6 beef or vegetable bouillon cubes
- 1 cup small pasta shells

Instructions:

1. Chop bacon and crisp it in a large stock pot at a medium heat.
2. Add all ingredients to the stock pot except for pasta shells. Be sure to drain and rinse the beans.
3. Simmer for 1½-2 hours.
4. Remove bay leaves.
5. Add pasta shells and simmer until tender.

Split Pea Soup

Cook Time: 3 hrs.

Ingredients:

- 3 cups dried yellow split peas (1 pound)
- 12 cups water
- 2 yellow onions, diced
- 4 stalks celery, diced
- 8-10 carrots, diced
- 1 large ham bone
- 1 - 1 ½ lbs. ham
- 1 tbl parsley flakes
- 1 tsp pepper
- 1 tbl garlic, minced

Instructions:

1. Place peas in a bowl and soak them in 4 cups of water until they are soft. Pick out discolored peas and skins that float.
2. Rinse peas and put them in a Dutch oven with 8 cups of water.
3. Boil uncovered for 2 minutes.
4. Turn off the stove and let stand for about 30 minutes.
5. Dice vegetables and ham and add to peas.
6. Stir in onions, celery, seasonings, and ham bone.
7. Bring to a quick boil, reduce heat to low, and simmer for 1 ½ hours.
8. Remove ham bone and cut any ham from the bone. Cut ham into small pieces and return ham to pot.
9. Cover and simmer for 30 minutes and serve.

Vegetable Beef

Cook Time: 1 hr.

Ingredients:

- 1 ½-2 lbs. beef chuck roast
- 2 tbls olive oil
- 2 tbls garlic, minced
- ½ tsp salt
- ½ tsp pepper
- 1 large onion, diced
- 1 tbl Worcestershire sauce
- ⅓ cup Merlot wine

- 8 cups beef broth
- 28 oz. diced tomatoes
- 2 tbls tomato paste
- 1 tbl Italian seasoning
- 3 cups potatoes, cubed
- 5 carrots, diced
- 2-3 celery stalks, diced
- 1 ½ cups green beans
- 1 ½ cups corn
- 1 ½ cups peas

Instructions:

1. Chop beef into small pieces and add to a large Dutch oven with olive oil, garlic, salt, and pepper.
2. Brown beef at a medium-high heat for about 4 minutes.
3. Stir in onion, Worcestershire sauce, and red wine. Cook for another 2 minutes.
4. Add broth, tomatoes with juices, tomato paste, and Italian seasoning. Simmer covered for 15 minutes.
5. Add potatoes, carrots, and celery. Simmer covered for 15 minutes.
6. Add green beans, corn, and peas. Simmer covered for 5-10 minutes until vegetables and beef are tender and serve.

Sides

Cheesy Potatoes

Temp: 375°F   **Cook Time:** 60 min.

Ingredients:

- 1 ½ cups sour cream
- 10.5 oz. cream of mushroom or chicken soup (p. 329)
- ¼ cup butter, melted
- ½ tbl garlic powder
- 1 tsp salt
- 2 cups cheddar cheese, shredded
- 2 lbs. frozen hashbrowns, thawed
- 1 cup cornflakes, crushed (optional)

Instructions:

1. Preheat oven to 375°F.
2. In a large bowl, combine sour cream, soup, butter, seasonings, and cheese.
3. Mix in thawed hashbrowns.
4. Spread out the hashbrown mixture into a 9x13" baking dish.
5. Sprinkle crushed cornflakes on top if desired.
6. Place in oven and cook for 60 minutes until top is golden.
7. Remove and serve.

Double Baked Potatoes

Temp: 375°F   **Cook Time:** 1 hr. 15 min.

Ingredients:

- 6 large russet potatoes
- ½ cup sour cream
- ¼ cup butter
- ¼ cup milk
- ½ tsp garlic powder
- 2 tsp salt
- 1 ½ cups cheddar cheese, shredded
- additional toppings if desired

Instructions:

1. Preheat oven to 375°F.
2. Wash, dry, and pierce potatoes.
3. Set on a foil-covered baking sheet and bake for 1 hour. Potatoes should be soft enough to easily stick a fork into.
4. Remove from oven and scoop out ¾ of the potato into a bowl shape, placing the scraped-out portions into a medium bowl.
5. With a hand mixer, blend potatoes with sour cream, butter, milk, garlic powder, salt, and half of the cheese.
6. Fill potato bowls with mashed potatoes and top with the remaining cheese.
7. Bake for another 15 minutes until the cheese is melted.
8. Add additional toppings if desired and serve.

Loaded Baked Potatoes

Temp: 425°F   **Cook Time:** 45 min.

Ingredients:

- 6 large russet potatoes
- olive oil
- salt
- 6 slices bacon
- 1 ½ cups broccoli, diced
- 6 tbls butter
- 1 ½ cups cheddar cheese, shredded
- sour cream

Instructions:

1. Preheat oven to 425°F.
2. Wash, dry, and pierce potatoes.
3. Brush potatoes with olive oil and dust them with salt. Set on a foil-lined baking sheet and bake for 45 minutes, or until potatoes are easily pierced with a fork.
4. While the potatoes are cooking, fry bacon in a large fry pan at a medium heat.
5. Crumble crispy bacon into a bowl.
6. Steam diced broccoli and place in another small bowl.
7. Remove the potatoes from the oven and fluff the interior of the potatoes.
8. Add 1 tbl of butter to each potato and divide the broccoli, bacon, and cheese between them. Top with sour cream.
9. Serve while warm.

Mashed Potatoes

Cook Time: 20 min.

Ingredients:

- 8 cups red or russet potatoes, chopped
- 12 cups water
- ½ cup sour cream
- ¼ cup milk
- ½ tsp garlic powder
- 2 tsp salt
- 6 tbls butter

Instructions:

1. If using red potatoes, wash and cube potatoes. If using russet, peel, wash, and cube potatoes.
2. Fill a large pot with water and bring to a boil. Then add potatoes.
3. Boil potatoes for 12-15 minutes. When potatoes are just soft enough to stick a fork into them, turn off the heat and drain potatoes.
4. Return the potatoes to the pot and add the remaining ingredients.
5. Beat with a hand mixer into a slightly chunky texture.
6. Scrape into a serving bowl and serve.

Oven Roasted Potatoes

Temp: 450°F   **Cook Time:** 30-40 min.

Ingredients:

- 3-4 lbs. red potatoes
- ⅓ cup olive oil
- 4 tbls butter, melted
- 2 tsp salt
- 1 tbl garlic, minced
- 1 tsp dried basil
- ¼ tsp pepper

Instructions:

1. Preheat oven to 450°F.
2. Wash potatoes and cut them into 1" chunks.
3. If you have time, soak the cut potatoes in cold water for at least an hour.
4. Drain potatoes and dry them thoroughly.
5. In a large bowl, toss potatoes with olive oil, butter, and spices.
6. Evenly distribute potatoes onto a foil-lined baking sheet.
7. Scrape out oil and spices from the bowl onto the potatoes.
8. Place the pan on the center rack of the oven and cook for 30 minutes or until the potatoes are tender and golden.
9. Remove from oven, transfer to a serving dish, and serve.

A Summer Afternoon

I paused from reading the epistle. Paul was writing the Thessalonians a word of encouragement. What an amusing thought. I looked across the bed at my patient listener. She was quiet, hopefully consumed with pleasant thoughts. I had been reading for most of the last hour since I arrived. My greeting was simple, and I got to reading right away. I only had so much time here, and I wanted to make sure I could finish this book today. But right now, my thoughts are elsewhere.

Summer had started to show her sunny face. To think, it was only Mother's Day a couple of short weeks ago. But now, June had arrived in full bloom. Now was the time for camping, family visits, swimming pools, and cookouts. Oh, how I missed those cookouts. Was it already a year since we'd had one? And a few weeks since we had all been together? But we are here together now. My audience of one waiting for me to continue. My mom.

Ahh, my mom. She wouldn't have participated much in the cooking part of the cookouts. I smile at this thought. Dad would have done more of that. I can't think about that now. But Mom would have made her potato salad. How I'd love to have some! That is what we should be doing this afternoon. We should be at the house, having hot dogs and watermelon and potato salad. Isn't that what summers are for?

But no. Not now. This summer is full of yellowed walls, IV drips, and musty food. I can smell antiseptic and hand sanitizer, and something I'd rather not acknowledge. And they are full of this, afternoons reading the New Testament. I pause a moment longer and movement catches my eye. I see a shoulder shift by the doorframe, a shoe just within sight. Someone is listening. I smile. Perhaps he is getting more out of my regular readings than my mother. I suppose it is not bad to have an active audience.

I go back to my chapter. But how can I read this? What hope is in these passages? Do I dare read them here, in this place? I continue reading, but my mind bounces between the present and prayer. Can she even hear me? How many heartbeats do I have left?

Drip, drip. The IV continues, and so must I. The man in the doorframe is still listening. Perhaps he can find comfort where I do not.

I finish the book, or this one anyway. There will be more tomorrow afternoon. Another day in this dismal place. Perhaps the sunshine of the kids will do her good. I close my Bible and return it to my purse. But I can't get up as my eyes drift back to my mother. Her face is still. Her hair is no longer dyed like it once was, now fine and frail. No helmet on her head, as Dad called her wigs. She is quiet. I never knew her like this. Mom was loud, full of energy. Not always good energy, but she lived life as she knew how. But closed lips have taken the place of her smile, and I struggle to remember the color of her eyes.

I look back at the monitor. Nothing moves but the steady rhythm of her heart and the IV. I rise to say my goodbyes, giving her one last kiss on the forehead before I go. Perhaps tomorrow, or the next will be the day. She will tell me to stop reading or to go just one more chapter. Maybe she'll remind me to grab something for the kids from the house on the way home. And maybe next summer we can have her potato salad, the only good food she made, with the whole family on an afternoon like this one.

Grandma's Potato Salad

Cook Time: 25 min.

Ingredients:

- 2 ½ lbs. potatoes (6-8 medium potatoes)
- ½ stalk celery
- ⅓ cup Vidalia onion
- 8 hard-boiled eggs
- ⅔ cup mayonnaise
- ½ tsp salt
- ½ tsp pepper
- ⅛ tsp garlic powder
- 2 tsp mustard
- 1 tsp sugar

Instructions:

1. Bring a large pot of water to a boil and add peeled and chopped potatoes.
2. Boil for 16 minutes. They should be cooked, but mostly firm.
3. Drain potatoes and add to a large bowl.
4. Dice the celery, onion, and six of the hard-boiled eggs. Add to the potatoes.
5. Add mayonnaise, salt, pepper, garlic powder, mustard, and sugar.
6. Mix until just combined.
7. Slice the remaining eggs and place them on top of the potato salad.
8. Serve now or chill for an hour before serving.

Scalloped Potatoes

Temp: 350°F, or 325°F   **Cook Time:** 30 min., or 2 hrs.

Ingredients:

- 5 medium potatoes
- 1 ¼ cups cheddar cheese, shredded
- ⅓ cup butter
- 1 cup milk
- 1 cup cornflake crumbs (optional)

Instructions:

1. Peel and slice potatoes.
2. Bring a large pot of water to a boil. Add potato slices and boil for 8 minutes, or until tender.
3. Drain and layer the sliced potatoes in a 9x13" baking dish.
4. Preheat oven to 350°F.
5. Melt together cheese, butter, and milk in a microwave-safe dish or saucepan, stirring regularly.
6. Pour the cheese mixture over the potatoes.
7. Add cornflakes if desired.
8. Bake in the oven for 30 minutes and serve.
    a. Alternatively: Place peeled and sliced potatoes into the casserole dish.
    b. Melt together the cheese mixture and pour over the potatoes.
    c. Cover and cook in the oven for 2 hours at 325°F.

Pierogi

Ingredients:

Dough
- 3 cups flour
- 2 eggs, beaten
- 1 cup sour cream
- 1 tsp salt

- 2 ½ cups diced potatoes
- ¼ cup milk
- 1 tsp salt
- 3 tbls butter
- 1 cup cheddar cheese

Filling

Instructions:

1. Combine flour, eggs, sour cream, and salt in a bowl or mixer. Dough should be stiff, but elastic when you press it.
2. Roll into a ball and cover with plastic wrap. Set it aside.
3. Bring a large pot of water to a boil. Add potatoes and boil for 15-20 minutes until soft. If desired, boil with a garlic clove.
4. Drain potatoes and blend with milk, salt, and butter.
5. Place in fridge to cool. Once potatoes are cool, mix in cheese.
6. Take a large pot and bring 8 cups of water with salt to a boil.
7. Uncover the dough and divide it in two. Re-cover one half.
8. Roll dough out on a floured surface to a ¼" thick.
9. Use 3" cut n seal to cut out dough circles. Place 1-2 tbls of the potatoes in the center of the circles. This is best done with a cookie scoop. Fold dough into a semicircle and seal the edge.
10. Repeat with all the dough. This should make 26-28 pierogi.
11. Boil pierogi until they float. Place them on a cooling rack.
12. Fry drained pierogi until golden in butter or lard with onions.

Notes: You must boil pierogi to cook the raw egg in the dough before freezing or eating. Do not thaw unfried pierogi or store dough in the fridge for more than 2 days. To make kluski, roll to desired thickness, cut with a sharp knife, and boil.

Other Fillings

Loaded Potato Cheese

- 2½ lbs. potatoes
- 2 tbls butter
- ¼ cup sour cream
- ½ tsp pepper
- ½ tsp salt
- 4 oz. cheddar cheese, shredded
- ⅓ cup bacon, cooked and chopped (optional)

Sweet Cheese

- 1 lb. farmers cheese (or 8 oz. cream cheese + 16 oz. cottage cheese, drained)
- ¼ cup powdered sugar
- 1 tsp vanilla extract

With fruit:

- 1 tbl sweet cheese
- 3-4 fresh berries
- ½ strawberry, diced
- ½ canned sliced peaches, diced

Note: Cold fillings are much easier to work with.

Beef and Mushroom

- 1 lb. beef, cooked and minced
- 1 medium onion, diced
- 4 oz. mushrooms, diced
- ⅓ cup sour cream
- 2 cloves garlic, minced
- ½ tsp pepper
- ½ tsp salt

Rueben

- 2 ½ cups corned beef, cooked and minced
- ½ lb. sauerkraut
- ½ cup thousand island dressing
- 1 ½ oz. Swiss cheese, shredded (optional)
- 1 tsp caraway, ground

Kapusta

- 2 lbs. sauerkraut
- 1 medium onion, diced

- ⅓ lb. bacon, cooked and chopped
- 4 oz. smoked kielbasa, minced
- 1-2 tbls brown sugar
- ⅓ cup sour cream (optional)

Afternoon Talks

Roll. Press. Scoop. Fold.

"So anyway, that's what I thought about his speech. Fine sounding, but the arguments were just talking points. No substance, no heart."

I hand another sealed pierogi to my brother, and he stirs the pot around. One from a few minutes ago floats to the top, and he scoops it out and lays it on the rack to dry, nodding at my comments. "I'd have to agree, but '*Let me be clear…it can be…very difficult…to give a convincing speech.*'"

My mom and I both laugh at my brother, his accent spot on, his mannerisms a mirror of their subject. True to form, he performs the same speech we just listened to, only this one is much more honest and comical.

Roll. Press. Scoop. Fold.

My mom shakes her head, rolling her eyes. "Ok, but what about school? What did you say your professor talked about yesterday?"

I dust my hands with flour as my mom and brother banter back and forth about some nonsense or other from the college prof. I go to interject, but the moment has passed. I finish pressing the next seven pierogi just as my brother is removing the last of the previous batch. He drops them in gently so as to not splash the boiling water and adds some more salt, stirring the mixture slightly.

"Hey, did I tell you guys about the latest piece we're reading in class?" They shake their heads and listen as I give a quick recounting of the tale. We laugh, marveling at the absurdity of the characters, yet we are somehow still somber, recognizing current events.

Roll. Press. Scoop. Fold.

Our assembly line continues. Perhaps we're not as efficient as some (I doubt Ford would hire us at this point), but we make do. After all, it is not just about the dough, or the potatoes, or watching the stove. My brother carries another tray downstairs, exchanging it for the one in the freezer. My mom pulls out the freezer bags and counts out 36 to store for a future meal, commenting on a story she heard on the news earlier that day, asking for our thoughts. Yes, there are certainly faster ways to do this. But what would be the fun of that?

Roll. Press. Scoop. Fold.

The last batch is almost done, and my brother pulls out a new pan. He cuts a few tablespoons of butter and starts to melt it, forming a nice puddle in the bottom of the pan. Plop, plop, plop. The last pierogi are boiling, and we eagerly wait and watch, watch and wait. This is the best part of pierogi day: the eating. After all, we have to make sure they taste good. My mom takes a few dried pierogi and browns each side in the simmering butter. I can practically taste them, but first I have to finish cleaning. The conversation continues at an easy pace, the sun slowly setting.

"Soup's on!" My mom starts portioning out pierogi and sour cream on our plates and we lean against the counter to finish our conversation.

"So, are you really going to wait to start that project?"

"How is your sister doing?"

"When is the next concert?"

"Yeah, my car is hanging in there."

"Can you pick them up next week?"

We eat and savor and clean. Tomorrow, we will have one more day together. In two days, we will go our separate ways, collecting more stories for the following weekend. But for now, we are here, finishing bits of fried dough and boisterous conversation as we wait for my dad to get home. My mom starts rustling something together. Looks like it'll be ham tonight with our pierogi. I move to the living room and my brother follows, mentioning something about a paper he has to start that's due next week. I roll my eyes, but smile, welcoming the conversation for the few minutes it lasts.

Potato Chips

Temp: 380°F   **Cook Time:** 20 min.

Ingredients:

- 3 large russet potatoes
- 2 tbls vinegar
- 1 qt. water, cold
- 2 tsp salt
- olive or canola oil

Instructions:

1. Peel, wash, and slice potatoes to about 1/16" thick. This is best done on a mandolin slicer.
2. Fill a medium bowl with cold water and add the vinegar.
3. Soak the potatoes in water for 20 minutes.
4. Drain potatoes in a colander and rinse them off in the sink.
5. Pat potatoes dry.
6. Heat 3" of oil in a deep and wide pot to 380°F.
7. Fry potato slices in small batches so they do not stick together.
8. When they are golden, remove from the pan.
9. Drain fried chips on a cooling rack above a baking pan, dust with salt, and serve.

Placki (Potato Pancakes)

Cook Time: 20 min.

Ingredients:

- 4 large potatoes (4 cups shredded)
- 1 small yellow onion
- 1 egg
- 1 tsp salt
- ½ tsp pepper
- 2-4 tbls flour
- butter, oil, or bacon grease
- sour cream

Instructions:

1. Peel and wash potatoes.
2. Finely grate potatoes and onion into a large bowl.
3. Squeeze the moisture out of the potatoes either through cheesecloth or a sifter.
4. Mix in egg, salt, and pepper. Gradually add enough flour to make the mixture thick.
5. In a large fry pan, heat oil of choice to a medium heat.
6. Add ¼ cup of potatoes into the pan and flatten to about ½" thick.
7. Fry, turning once, until both sides are golden brown.
8. Transfer to a paper towel lined plate to drain.
9. Repeat until all potato mixture is used. Add more frying oil as needed.
10. Serve hot with sour cream.

Learning From the Best

The potatoes were brown to begin with.

This was her first time making these, but she was sure she could do it. After all, she'd seen Dad do it countless times. You shred potatoes, mix the stuff together, and fry them in butter. And he was here, vaguely helping in the background. How hard could it be? But here she was halfway through, and before her sat a pile of mushy, slimy, brown potatoes.

Sigh. This was not how they looked when Dad made them. Dejected, she threw them into the trash.

But as it is in such scenarios, timing is everything. At that moment, her dad turned and saw what she had done. Being the stoic type, he took stock of the situation first. He saw the flour and eggs on the counter, the salt and pepper next to the bowl. Some butter now browning in the hot pan. An onion just diced. And a pile of potato peels in the sink with no shredded potatoes to show for it.

"Joey, what are you doing?"

Exasperated, she replied, "I'm making potato pancakes!"

"Well," he gestured around the kitchen, "where are the potatoes?"

With a huff, she pulled the trash can over to show her dad. "They turned brown, so I threw them away."

"Why would you do that? Potatoes always turn brown! They're fine!"

This was a surprise. She had seen her father make these countless times. So, she watched him make them again. Her father, the experienced cook, shredded the potatoes much faster this time. No brown potatoes. But he let them sit, just to show her that yes, potatoes do get brown, and yes, they are quite fine to eat.

By this time, she was quite convinced. But, because he was here anyway, they finished making this favorite snack together. Just to make sure. After all, you can't be too sure with brown potatoes, and it's nice to have an expert.

Baked Sweet Potatoes

Temp: 425°F   **Cook Time:** 1 hr.

Ingredients:

- 6 sweet potatoes
- olive oil
- 6 tbls dark brown sugar
- 1 tbl ground cinnamon
- 6 tbls butter, melted

Instructions:

1. Preheat oven to 425°F.
2. Wash and dry sweet potatoes. Prick them with a fork or knife and brush them with olive oil.
3. Place sweet potatoes on a foil-covered baking sheet and bake for 1 hour. A fork should easily pierce them when done.
4. A few minutes before sweet potatoes finish baking, combine brown sugar, cinnamon, and butter in a small bowl.
5. Remove sweet potatoes from the oven and let them sit for a few minutes to cool.
6. Slice sweet potatoes open and fluff the insides with a fork.
7. Divide brown sugar mixture evenly between potatoes and serve.

Sweet Potato Fries

Temp: 350°F   **Cook Time:** 30 min.

Ingredients:

- 1 large sweet potato
- ⅓ cup cornstarch
- ⅓ cup club soda
- canola oil
- 1 tbl sugar
- ½ tsp ground cinnamon

Instructions:

1. Peel and slice sweet potatoes into ¼" thick fries.
2. Whisk cornstarch and club soda in a medium bowl.
3. Heat a medium saucepan with 2" of oil to 350°F.
4. Dip the fries into the cornstarch mixture and then gently place them in the oil.
5. Fry for 2 minutes, drain, dip back into the cornstarch mixture, and then fry again until they begin to turn brown.
6. Drain on a paper towel, dust with cinnamon sugar, and serve.
   a. Alternatively, dust sliced sweet potatoes with 1 tbl of cornstarch and toss with ¼ cup olive oil. Bake one baking sheet at a time for 30 minutes at 450°F, turning the fries halfway through. Remove from oven and dust with cinnamon sugar or salt.

Sweet Potato Casserole

Temp: 425°F, 350°F

Cook Time: 1 hr. 30 min.

Ingredients:

- 4 lbs. sweet potatoes
- ½ cup butter, melted
- ½ cup heavy cream
- 2 eggs, beaten
- 2 tsp vanilla extract
- ¾ cup brown sugar
- 2 tsp ground cinnamon
- ½ tsp ground nutmeg
- ½ tsp salt

Topping

- ¾ cup rolled oats
- ½ cup flour
- 1 cup brown sugar
- ½ cup chopped pecans
- 6 tbls butter, softened
- 1 tsp ground cinnamon
- ¼ tsp salt

Instructions:

1. Preheat oven to 425°F.
2. Wash sweet potatoes, puncture them multiple times with a knife or fork, wrap in foil, place on parchment lined baking sheet, and cook for 40 minutes-1 hour until tender.
3. Remove from oven and let cool before removing skins.
4. Place skinless sweet potatoes into a food processor and blend smooth. Add to a large mixing bowl.
5. Add remaining ingredients and combine until smooth.
6. Pour the mixture into a large, greased baking dish. Lower oven temperature to 350°F.
7. In a small bowl, blend topping ingredients to a coarse texture.
8. Sprinkle topping on sweet potato mixture evenly.
9. Bake in the oven for 30 minutes until the topping is lightly browned. Then remove and serve.

Creamy Red Sauce Tortellini

Cook Time: 10 min.

Ingredients:

- 2 tbls olive oil
- 2 tbls garlic, minced
- 8 oz. tomato sauce
- 8 oz. tomato paste
- ¾ cup heavy cream
- 1 tsp salt
- 1 tsp dried basil
- 1 tsp brown sugar
- ½ cup parmesan cheese, grated
- 24 oz. fresh cheese tortellini
- 3 cups broth

Instructions:

1. Heat garlic in oil in a large frypan at a medium heat for 2 minutes.
2. Add tomato sauce, heavy cream, spices, and brown sugar.
3. Simmer for 5 minutes.
4. Stir in parmesan and reduce heat to low.
5. In a medium saucepan, boil tortellini in broth for 4-5 minutes and drain any remaining liquid.
6. Once the tortellini are done, add to the sauce, stir together, and serve.

Crumble Noodles

Cook Time: 20 min.

Ingredients:

- 2 ½ cups water
- 2 tbls better than bouillon chicken base
- 16 oz. thin egg noodles

Butter Sauce

- ¼ cup leftover broth
- 4 tbls butter

Crumble Topping

- 3 tbls butter
- 1 tsp parsley
- 12 crushed ritz crackers

Instructions:

1. Bring the water and better than bouillon to a boil in a medium saucepan.
2. Add egg noodles and boil for about 7-9 minutes until they are tender.
3. Drain the leftover broth into a small mixing bowl. Set noodles in a warmed serving dish.
4. For the sauce, take a ¼ cup of the broth and mix with 4 tbls of butter. If needed, melt the butter fully in a saucepan or microwave.
5. For the crumble topping, sauté butter, parsley, and crushed crackers in a small fry pan at a medium-low heat for about 4 minutes until the crackers are golden.
6. Pour the butter sauce over the noodles, top with the crackers, and serve.

Parmesan Noodles

Cook Time: 20 min.

Ingredients:

- 16 oz. fettuccine or wide egg noodles
- 1 tbl olive oil
- 5 tbls butter
- ¾ cup parmesan cheese, grated
- ½ tsp salt
- 1 tsp garlic powder

Instructions:

1. Bring a large pot of water to a boil.
2. Add noodles and cook for about 8 minutes until tender.
3. Melt butter in a large frypan.
4. Drain noodles and stir in 1 tbl of olive oil.
5. Add noodles to the frypan and turn heat to low.
6. Stir in parmesan, salt, and garlic powder.
7. Once everything is combined, remove from heat and serve in a warmed and covered serving dish.

Fried Apples

Cook Time: 30 min.

Ingredients:

- ¼ cup butter
- 2 lbs. apples (6 medium, 7 cups sliced)
- 2 cups apple cider or water, divided
- 3 tsp cornstarch
- 3 tbls brown sugar
- ¼ cup sugar
- 2 tsp ground cinnamon
- ¼ tsp ground nutmeg
- 1 tsp lemon juice
- ½ tsp vanilla extract

Instructions:

1. Melt butter in a medium fry pan.
2. Core and slice apples and place them in the pan with 1 cup of apple juice or water.
3. Sauté apples at a medium heat for 5 minutes until they are tender.
4. Add sugars, spices, lemon juice, and vanilla to the pan.
5. In a small bowl, whisk cornstarch with the remaining liquid.
6. Add cornstarch and liquid to the pan and stir until the juice is thick and smooth.
7. Remove from heat and serve alone or with cornbread.
    a. Alternatively, toss apples in the cornstarch and place them in a crock pot. Whisk together the remaining ingredients and add to the apples. Cover and cook on HIGH for 3 hours or LOW for 6 hours.

Corn Casserole

Temp: 350°F   **Cook Time:** 40-45 min.

Ingredients:

- 6 tbls butter, softened
- ½ cup sugar
- 15 oz. whole kernel corn, drained
- 15 oz. creamed corn
- 1 cup sour cream
- 2 eggs, beaten
- 1 cup cornmeal
- ½ cup flour
- 1 tbl baking powder
- ½ tsp salt

Instructions:

1. Preheat oven to 350°F.
2. In a large bowl, combine softened butter with the sugar.
3. Add corn, sour cream, and eggs.
4. In a small bowl, whisk together cornmeal, flour, baking powder, and salt.
5. Add dry ingredients to wet ingredients and stir until just combined.
6. Grease a 9" square baking dish and pour the batter in.
7. Bake in the oven for 35-40 minutes.
8. Once the center has set, remove the pan from the oven and serve immediately.

Acorn Squash

Temp: 350°F   **Cook Time:** 1 hr.

Ingredients:

- 2 acorn squashes
- 8 tbls brown sugar
- 4 tbls butter

Instructions:

1. Preheat oven to 350°F.
2. Cut squashes in half, scrape out seeds and fibers, and place them cut sides down onto a buttered baking sheet.
3. Place in oven for 30 minutes.
4. Remove from oven, flip squashes cut side up, and add butter and brown sugar evenly to each squash half.
5. Return to oven and bake for another 30 minutes, or until flesh is tender.
6. Remove from oven and combine squash with butter and brown sugar. The result will look something like applesauce.
7. Serve in the squash shells or scoop into a serving dish.

Candied Carrots

Cook Time: 10 min.

Ingredients:

- 1 lb. baby carrots
- ½ cup water
- ¼ cup butter
- ¼ cup brown sugar
- ½ tsp ground cinnamon
- ¼ tsp salt

Instructions:

1. Bring carrots, water, butter, and brown sugar to a quick boil in a small saucepan.
2. Reduce to a low simmer and cover for 5 minutes.
3. Uncover the pan and add cinnamon and salt.
4. Bring heat to medium and stir until the glaze has reduced and the carrots are tender, about another 5 minutes.
5. Remove from heat and spoon into a serving dish.

Corn on the Cob

Cook Time: 10 min.

Ingredients:

- 10 cups water
- 2 tbls sugar
- ½ cup milk
- 2 tbls butter
- 8 ears of corn

Instructions:

1. Bring water, sugar, milk, and butter to a boil in a large stock pot.
2. Peel leaves and silk from corn and cut cobs in half, if desired.
3. Add corn, cover, and bring back to a boil.
4. After 2 minutes, reduce heat to the lowest setting and let the corn simmer for another 7 minutes.
5. Remove corn cobs and serve.

Roasted Brussels Sprouts

Temp: 400°F   **Cook Time:** 20 min.

Ingredients:

- 1 lb. Brussels sprouts
- 2 tbls garlic, minced
- 2 tsp salt
- ¼ cup olive oil
- ¼ cup parmesan cheese, grated

Instructions:

1. Preheat oven to 400°F.
2. Wash Brussels sprouts and slice them in half vertically.
3. Add sprouts to a medium bowl and toss in garlic, salt, olive oil, and parmesan.
4. Spread sprouts on a 9x13" glass baking pan and cook in the oven for 20 minutes, turning sprouts regularly so they cook evenly. They should look golden on the edges when they are done.
5. Remove from oven and spoon into a serving dish.

Onion Rings

Temp: 375-400°F   **Cook Time:** 10 min.

Ingredients:

- 1 large Vidalia onion
- 1 egg
- 8 oz. beer or ginger ale
- 1 ½ cups flour
- 1 tsp baking powder
- 1 tsp garlic powder
- 1 tsp salt
- ¾ cup breadcrumbs (optional)
- olive or canola oil

Instructions:

1. Remove the skin from the onion and cut off the root. Slice onion into ¼" slices.
2. Set onion slices in a bowl of ice water for 1 hour.
3. Heat 2" of oil in a deep saucepan to 375-400°F.
4. In a small bowl, mix the egg, beer, flour, baking powder, garlic powder, and salt.
5. Dip onion rings into the batter mixture and, if desired, into breadcrumbs.
6. Carefully set battered onion rings into the hot oil, but not so many that they touch while frying.
7. Once the batter is lightly browned, remove rings with a skimmer or tongs, drain on a cookie rack above a paper towel, and serve hot.

Hard-boiled Eggs

Ingredients:

- 6-12 eggs, preferably one or two weeks old
- water
- ½ tsp salt
- ice cubes

Instructions:

1. Take a medium-sized saucepan and place 6 eggs in the bottom of the pan. Fill with water until the eggs are covered with 1" of water. If you want to make 12 hard-boiled eggs, use either a wider pot or fill to 2" above the eggs.
2. Add the salt to the water and quickly bring to a rolling boil.
3. Once the water is at that roiling boil, immediately turn the stove off and cover the pot.
4. Let the eggs sit in the pot for 10 minutes. If you like a softer egg, let them sit for 6 minutes. For a harder egg, 12-15.
5. Strain the eggs from the hot water and run them under cold water. For better results, then add them to a bowl of ice water. Cracking the eggs a little as they sit in the ice water can also help.
6. Once they are cool to the touch, you can peel the eggs.
7. Unpeeled eggs last about five days in the refrigerator; peeled eggs last about two days.

(Dragoned) Deviled Eggs

Ingredients:

- 12 hard-boiled eggs
- ⅓ cup mayonnaise
- ¼ tsp salt
- 1 ½ tbls Dijon mustard
- paprika (optional)

Instructions:

1. Slice the hard-boiled eggs in half lengthwise and pop the yolks into a medium bowl.
2. Mash the yolks and mix in the mayonnaise, salt, and mustard.
3. Scrape yolk filling into a star-tipped piping bag and pipe filling into the hollows of the egg whites.
4. Dust with paprika if desired and serve.

Pizza Chicken and Dragoned Eggs

Do you have any phrases or words that seem to come from only your family? Perhaps you say things like dupa, or siéntete, or thingamajig. Or…perhaps you're normal. (Or boring, I don't know). What I do know is that my family has come up with a number of names for items and foods that don't really make sense. My brother Josh and I can use hand motions and vague sounds to communicate, and somehow, we will still know what the other is talking about (even when we have yet to find the word). And we also have names for things that only make sense in context. My youngest brother is Oejay because Josh and I learned Pig Latin at an opportune time. Josh of course is Oshkosh because it rhymes. I'm Matt, although I couldn't tell you why. And then, there are names for things in the kitchen. Like shoe polish for Kitchen Bouquet, pizza chicken for chicken parmesan, and the famous dragoned eggs.

Yes, those names arose out of necessity. See, my mother did not raise picky eaters, and yet we still had one. And to him, everything was chicken. Pork chops, turkey, steak, roast, and of course, chicken. But how do you convince a child of this? Well…you don't. You simply don't correct their mistake. And so, my brother, upon seeing the sauce and cheese-covered chicken on his plate promptly called it pizza chicken (pizza was another favorite). As we did not want to dissuade him from eating dinner, we did not correct him. Thus, our own vocabulary changed.

But a different route was taken with the dragoned eggs. Like many evangelical families, we could not be too careful about the words passing our tongues. So, in order to better season our speech, my mother concocted the perfect substitute for the devil: dragons. Now at the time, my biggest complaint with this word was that I loved dragons. Dearly. I thought they were the coolest things since dolphins. I wanted a pet dragon, drew them on every other sheet of paper, and even wrote a story about one. How could we be eating these precious creatures? But no, dragon was much better than devil, my mom said. Looking back, I cannot help but laugh at this choice. For in utilizing the name dragon, she simply used a euphemism for the devil, and there is a certain irony in that.

But why else do we call things what they are? Do you know why deviled eggs are called thus? Because they have been grilled and are served with hot toppings. And as hell is hot…so named are the eggs. One might think of devil's food cake as well. While not hot, it does serve as an amusing contrast to angel food cake. But for our poor, misjudged eggs, there is nothing particularly devilish about them. They are just spicy! And so, where we once called things by what they were made with, now we call things by what they are not.

Yet these are the terms I still hear in my family's house today. Along with pizza chicken and shoe polish, these nicknames make me laugh. I keep them (most of them) with my children today. And this is not always intentional. Sometimes I catch myself saying to one child, "Get your dupa over here." My vocabulary has been permanently altered, as does happen with language. But other times, I keep the names for remembrance's sake, like these silly food names, because they remind me of my family. And what is better than food, family, and memories?

Cheesy Rice

Cook Time: 20 min.

Ingredients:

- 1 ½ cups basmati rice
- 3 cups broth
- 3 tbls butter
- 1 tsp onion powder
- 1 tsp garlic powder
- ¼ tsp salt
- 1 ½ cups cheddar cheese, shredded
- ¼ cup sour cream

Instructions:

1. Boil rice in the broth until all the broth is absorbed.
2. In a large fry pan, melt butter at a low heat and add seasonings.
3. Stir rice into the butter.
4. Add cheese and sour cream and thoroughly incorporate.
5. Scrape into a medium-sized serving bowl and serve.

Fried Rice

Cook Time: 30 min.

Ingredients:

- 1 cup white rice
- 1 ½ cups water
- 2 tbls olive oil
- ¼ cup corn
- ¼ cup peas
- ½ cup carrots, diced
- ½ tbl garlic, minced
- ½ tsp salt
- 2 tbls soy sauce
- 1 egg, beaten

Instructions:

1. Boil rice in water until all the water is absorbed. This should take 15-20 minutes.
2. Add olive oil to a large pan and, at a medium heat, sauté garlic for 1 minute.
3. Add vegetables and salt to the pan and cook until the carrots are soft. This should take about 8 minutes.
4. Beat the egg in a small bowl and mix it with the vegetables to make scrambled eggs.
5. Add the rice and soy sauce to the pan, stir together, and serve.

Brassica Salad

Ingredients:

- 2 cups Asian broccoli, chopped
- 4 cups Napa cabbage, shredded
- 1 cup carrot
- ½ cup radish
- 1 cup yellow squash
- 1 large red cabbage leaf

Dressing

- ½ cup mayonnaise
- ½ cup milk
- ⅓ cup sugar or honey
- 1 tbl red wine vinegar
- ¼ cup lemon juice
- ½ cup dried cranberries
- ½ cup sunflower seeds
- ½ cup pumpkin seeds
- ½ cup chickpeas, drained and rinsed

Instructions:

1. Finely shred broccoli, cabbage (this can be any type or combination of cabbage), carrot, radish, squash, and red cabbage leaf. Add to a large bowl.
2. In a small bowl, combine mayonnaise, milk, sugar, red wine vinegar, and lemon juice.
3. Pour dressing over the cabbage and stir everything together.
4. Set in the refrigerator for 1 hour.
5. Mix in cranberries, sunflower seeds, pumpkin seeds, and chickpeas.
6. Serve with sliced chicken and feta cheese.

Broccoli Salad

Ingredients:

- 8 cups broccoli
- ¼ cup red onion
- 1 lb. crisp bacon
- 1 cup dried cranberries
- 1 cup almonds, sliced

Dressing

- 1 cup mayonnaise
- ½ cup white sugar
- 2 tbls white wine vinegar

Instructions:

1. Dice broccoli, onion, and bacon. Toss in a large bowl with dried cranberries and almonds.
2. In a medium bowl, whisk together the dressing ingredients.
3. Pour dressing over broccoli mixture and mix well.
4. Refrigerate for 1 hour and serve.

Coleslaw

Ingredients:

- ½ cup mayonnaise
- ¼ cup milk
- 1 ½ tbls lemon juice
- 1 tbl red wine vinegar
- 2 tbls sugar
- ½ tsp salt
- ¼ tsp pepper
- 8 cups shredded coleslaw mix

Instructions:

1. Combine dressing ingredients in a large bowl.
2. Add coleslaw mix and combine well.
3. Refrigerate for 1 hour and serve.

Kapusta (Sauerkraut)

Cook Time: 35 min.

Ingredients:

- ½ lb. bacon
- 32 oz. sauerkraut, rinsed
- ½ lb. smoked kielbasa
- ¼ cup brown sugar

Instructions:

1. Chop bacon and cook on medium in a large fry pan (do NOT drain the bacon grease).
2. Add rinsed sauerkraut to the pan with the cooked bacon.
3. Cook on low for 10 minutes.
4. Stir brown sugar into sauerkraut.
5. While sauerkraut is cooking, dice up kielbasa.
6. Add to the pan and cook for another 15 minutes.
7. Place in a serving dish and serve.

Cranberry Waldorf Salad

Ingredients:

- 1 ½ cups cranberries
- 1 cup red apple, chopped
- 1 cup celery, chopped
- 1 cup seedless grapes, sliced
- ⅓ cup raisins
- ¼ cups walnuts, chopped
- 2 tbls sugar
- ¼ tsp ground cinnamon
- 8 oz. vanilla yogurt

Instructions:

1. Combine all ingredients in a large bowl. Be sure that all ingredients are evenly coated.
2. Cover bowl and refrigerate for 2 hours before serving.

Pistachio Salad

Ingredients:

- 20 oz. crushed pineapple, drained
- 3 oz. instant pistachio pudding mix
- 8 oz. whipped cream
- 8 oz. mini marshmallows

Instructions:

1. Combine pineapple and pistachio mix in a large bowl.
2. Add whipped cream and marshmallows.
3. Refrigerate for 1 hour before serving.

Mandarin Orange Salad

Ingredients:

- ½ cup vegetable oil
- ¼ cup apple cider vinegar
- ¼ cup sugar
- 2 tsp dried parsley
- 1 tsp salt
- ⅛ tsp pepper
- ½ cup sliced almonds
- ¼ cup sugar
- 1 head red leaf lettuce, torn
- 1 red onion, chopped
- 1 cup chopped celery
- 22 oz. mandarin oranges, drained

Instructions:

1. In a jar or container with a lid, combine the oil, vinegar, sugar, and spices. Cover and shake well.
2. Refrigerate for at least 1 hour.
3. In a medium saucepan over a medium-low heat, toast and stir the almonds and sugar until the sugar has melted and the almonds are evenly coated.
4. Remove from heat, cool, and break apart.
5. Store at room temperature until ready to serve the salad.
6. In a large bowl, toss together the lettuce, celery, oranges, almonds, and dressing until evenly coated and serve.

Dips and Spreads

Bean Dip

Temp: 350°F

Cook Time: 25 min.

Ingredients:

- 16 oz. cream cheese
- 16 oz. refried beans
- ⅓ cup sour cream
- 1 tsp garlic powder
- 1 tsp salt

- ¼ tsp ground cumin
- ¼ tsp cayenne pepper
- 21 oz. Hormel chili
- 2 cups cheddar cheese
- 1 bag tortilla chips

Instructions:

1. Preheat oven to 350°F.
2. Spread cream cheese in a 9x13" baking dish.
3. Blend refried beans with sour cream and spices in a small bowl.
4. Spread beans evenly across the cream cheese.
5. Evenly layer beans with chili and top with cheddar cheese.
6. Heat in oven for 25 minutes, or until cheese is bubbly.
7. Remove from oven and serve with tortilla chips.

French Onion Dip

Ingredients:

- 8 oz. sour cream
- ½ tbl onion flakes
- 1 tsp onion powder
- ¼ tsp garlic powder
- ½ tbl chives
- 1 tsp parsley flakes
- ¼ tsp salt
- 1 tsp sugar
- ½ tsp lemon juice
- 1 tsp better than bullion beef or chicken paste

Instructions:

1. Mix all ingredients in a small bowl.
2. Cover and refrigerate for 2 hours before serving.

Hot Chipped Beef Dip

Temp: 350°F   **Cook Time:** 20 min.

Ingredients:

- ¼ cup onion, chopped
- 3 tbls butter
- ½ tbl Worcestershire sauce
- ½ cup sour cream
- 12 oz. cream cheese
- 3 oz. dried beef
- ½ cup pecans, chopped
- ½ tsp garlic powder
- ½ tsp salt

Instructions:

1. Preheat oven to 350°F.
2. In a large fry pan, sauté onion in butter at a medium-low heat.
3. Mix and melt the remaining ingredients in the pan.
4. Scrape everything into an 8" round baking dish.
5. Bake for 20 minutes and serve with crackers.

Salsa

Ingredients:

- 4 cups tomatoes, diced
- 8 oz. tomato paste
- 1 ½ tbls vinegar
- 1 tbl garlic, minced
- 2 small onions, diced
- 5 jalapeno peppers, diced
- ½ green pepper, diced
- 2 tbls cilantro, minced
- 1 tsp salt

Instructions:

1. Combine all ingredients in a medium bowl.
2. Cover and refrigerate until ready to serve.

Spinach and Water Chestnut Dip

Ingredients:

- 10 oz. spinach, chopped
- 16 oz. sour cream
- 1 cup mayonnaise
- 2 oz. dry vegetable soup mix
- 8 oz. water chestnuts, drained and chopped
- 3 green onions, chopped

Instructions:

1. Blend all ingredients in a medium bowl.
2. Cover and refrigerate for 2 hours before serving.

Garlic Toum

Ingredients:

- 1 cup garlic cloves
- 1 tsp salt
- ¼ cup lemon juice
- 4 cups extra light olive oil

Instructions:

1. Blend garlic and salt in a food processor. Slowly drizzle in and alternate lemon juice and oil over 10 minutes, adding in the oil ½ cup at a time in order to emulsify the oil.
2. Once smooth, scrape into a serving bowl and serve.

Garlic Dip

Ingredients:

- 1 cup mayonnaise
- 1 cup sour cream
- ⅓ cup garlic, minced
- 1 pinch parsley flakes

Instructions:

1. Mix all ingredients in a small bowl.
2. Refrigerate for 1 hour and serve.

Guacamole

Ingredients:

- 1 large avocado
- 1 clove garlic, minced
- 1 tbl red onion, chopped
- 1 tbl cilantro, chopped
- 1 tsp lime juice
- 1 pinch cayenne pepper
- 1 pinch salt

Instructions:

1. Cut the avocado in half and set aside the pit.
2. Scoop avocado flesh out of the skin into a medium bowl.
3. Mash avocado until it has a somewhat chunky texture.
4. Mix remaining ingredients with avocado until well combined.
5. Add pit to the middle of the guacamole mixture, cover the bowl, and refrigerate until ready to serve.

Hummus

Ingredients:

- 30 oz. chickpeas/garbanzo beans, drained and rinsed
- 6 tbls olive oil
- 2 tsp tahini
- 2 tsp salt
- 4 tbls garlic, minced

Instructions:

1. Drain and rinse chickpeas and add to a large food processor.
2. Grind to a fine paste, or to desired consistency.
3. Add half of the olive oil, tahini, salt, and garlic.
4. Combine thoroughly.
5. Taste. If the taste or consistency is not to your liking, you can add more of an ingredient you feel is insufficient. But add additional ingredients slowly. The flavors will become more pronounced once the hummus has been allowed to rest.
6. Let the hummus sit in the refrigerator to rest for 2 hours.
7. Remove from refrigerator and serve with pita or vegetables.

Too Much Garlic

I decided long ago that before you start a recipe, you should always be sure you have all of your ingredients before beginning. I do not mean that you should briefly glance at your cupboards and then start mixing. I mean get out every. Single. Ingredient. Line them up, double-check, then proceed.

My mom was preparing to cater an event for one of her friends. Thinking back, I cannot remember exactly who or what it was for. A bridal shower? Baby shower? Retirement party? But whoever it was, they asked for hummus and pita as part of the spread, and I had recently discovered and modified my own hummus recipe. This was for two reasons. 1) I was in college by that point and 2) I needed cheap and lasting meals to take with me throughout the day, and nut bars were not cutting it. So, hummus it was.

I often helped my mom prepare for these sorts of events. As the saying goes, many hands make light work, and by this point, my mom and I had become more used to each other in the kitchen. And it was good company. And not homework.

Now, hummus is not a complicated recipe. It is chickpeas, olive oil, a bit of tahini, salt, and garlic. I don't even measure anymore when I make it, a habit (or talent, depending on how you look at it) I inherited from my mother. Such was the case tonight.

Well, let me rephrase that. *I* was measuring everything because at the time I was compulsive about measuring. *My mother* was measuring nothing.

While I was making the hummus, my mother was making the pita bread. And my, did it smell delicious. But as I was finishing the hummus, I realized I needed that final ingredient: garlic. I had some pre-minced garlic already, but as came the taste test (which you always must have when cooking) I noted that there was not enough garlic.

"Hey, mom."

"Yes?"

"I need more garlic. Is there more in the fridge?"

We both check. It is all gone.

But my mother, the industrious one, said, "No biggie, I have some garlic cloves right here."

I stare at them dubiously, the mixer running in the background. "Well, how much should I use? I only need a tablespoon or two."

My mother looks at the cloves. "I'm assuming one or two cloves should work. That's about a couple of tablespoons, I would think."

Now, dear reader, refer yourself to the title of this piece. A little more couldn't hurt, right?

Wrong.

We peeled the garlic. We diced the garlic. We stuck it in the mixer with the rest of the ingredients, blending it smooth. Then came the fun part: the taste test.

I will have you know that, had these been normal, small garlic cloves, my mom's idea probably would have worked. Or perhaps if we had started small and worked our way up. But we had very large garlic, and we used what we presumed would equal two tablespoons of minced garlic.

So we took some of that nice warm bread, spread the hummus so smooth on top, and prepared to enjoy one of our favorite snacks. And then we burned our mouths.

Many people have said that garlic is like butter: you can't have too much. But I will tell you, dear reader, you *can* have too much garlic. Needless to say, we had to add so many more chickpeas to dilute the taste that we ended up making enough hummus for about two and a half events. I think we finished off most of it. But we learned our lesson: prepare before you bake, and a little more can hurt.

Burned Garlic Butter

Ingredients:

- ½ cup butter
- ¼ tsp garlic powder
- ½ tsp salt

Instructions:

1. In a medium frypan, heat butter on medium until the butter has turned a golden brown, stirring continually.
2. Fill a medium bowl with ice water. Set a small bowl inside.
3. Pour the butter into the small bowl and add seasonings.
4. Quickly whisk the butter until it begins to solidify. Once it is mostly solidified, scrape it into a serving dish.
5. Add to French bread or dinner rolls.

Honey Butter

Ingredients:

- ¼ cup butter, softened
- 2 ½ tbls honey
- 1 tbl powdered sugar
- ¼ tsp ground cinnamon

Instructions:

1. Add ingredients to a medium mixing bowl.
2. Whip ingredients at a medium speed with a hand mixer. Everything should be evenly distributed and the butter fluffy.
3. Scrape into a small serving bowl and add to rolls or toast.

Sauces and Fillings

What's in a Name?

There was nothing quite like cooking with Dad. He was a master in the kitchen. He knew all the spices, the proper temperatures, and all the right ways to mix and create. There was never a recipe to be seen, yet he always knew what to do. But there was one problem: you could never trust the names he gave for things when you asked while he was busy.

It was a lot like when he was gardening, you see. Dad loved to garden. He did it most days when he was home from work. Gardening was quiet, simple, caring. Plants do not shout or demand, or really do much of anything except exist for the simple pleasure of beauty. They took time and care, light and water. But if ever I should ask for a name of what Dad was planting, I'd get a name, but you could never tell if it was the right one. But it'd have a name.

Perhaps that was all he could come up with when one small nine-year-old constantly asked questions. What is this flower? How tall does this vine grow? When will this tree have peaches? And so on. Perhaps he knew I just needed an answer, even if it wasn't correct.

Such it was when he cooked. Everything had a name, and perhaps it was just more personal to him. And so, when I watched him make gravy, standing at his elbow as he whisked all the ingredients together, I asked what they were.

"What are you putting in now?"

"Flour."

"Why?"

"Because gravy needs to be thick, doesn't it?"

I watched a little longer as he added more drippings from a roast pan and then pulled out a brown bottle with a yellow lid. Out came a sticky, black liquid that hardly looked like something belonging in a kitchen, let alone a recipe.

"What…is that?"

My dad must have seen my scrunched nose and heard the hesitation in my voice. I didn't see him smile, but I am sure he did.

"Why, this here is shoe polish."

That couldn't be right. "Shoe polish?"

"Yes, shoe polish."

"…why?"

"Because you can't have a good gravy be too light. It always needs a bit of color in it. So, shoe polish."

I could not believe my eyes or my ears. Maybe my dad had finally lost it. But I continued to watch anyway, observing how the shoe polish did in fact add good color to the gravy like he said it would. It certainly looked like his normal gravy, and after stealing a taste, it certainly tasted like it. Satisfied, I ceased asking questions. Looking back, I wonder if perhaps my dad got tired of saying Kitchen Bouquet. So, when you go to make some gravy, do add a little shoe polish. You will not be disappointed.

Beef Gravy

Cook Time: 8 min.

Ingredients:

- 2 tbls butter
- 2 tbls flour
- 1 cup beef broth
- 2 tsp Kitchen Bouquet or Worcestershire sauce
- ¼ tsp salt

Instructions:

1. Melt butter in a medium saucepan.
2. Whisk in flour until well incorporated and cook at a medium heat for 2 minutes.
3. Slowly pour in the broth, whisking continually, and add the Worcestershire sauce and salt.
    a. You can also use chicken broth, or the drippings left over from a roast.
4. Simmer until gravy has thickened to your desired consistency and then remove from heat.
5. Add to a warmed gravy dish and serve.

Pizza or Pasta Sauce

Cook Time: 1 hr.

Ingredients:

- 3 tbls olive oil
- 3 tbls garlic, minced
- 12 oz. tomato paste
- 30 oz. tomato sauce
- 28 oz. crushed tomatoes
- 2 tbls sugar
- 1 tsp better than bullion chicken paste
- 1 ½ lbs. lean ground meat (optional)
- ½ tsp pepper
- 1 tsp salt
- 1 tsp onion powder
- 1 tsp parsley flakes
- ½ tbl dried oregano
- ½ tbl dried basil

Instructions:

1. Sauté garlic in olive oil in the bottom of a large stock pot at a medium-high heat for 4 minutes.
2. Add remaining ingredients and simmer for 45 minutes, or until sauce is at the desired thickness.
3. Remove from heat.
4. If desired, blend in a food processor or with an immersion blender for a smoother sauce.
5. When making a meat sauce for spaghetti or lasagna, brown ground meat in a fry pan, drain grease, and add to the sauce after the sauce is done cooking.
6. Makes 8 cups before adding meat.
7. Serve immediately, or cool and refrigerate or freeze.

The Evidence Remained to be Seen

The evidence remained to be seen of our poor choices. Red splatter covered every inch. It even made its way to the ceiling, but not before making stops on the counters and cupboards first. Even months later we were finding its remains in the grout between floor tiles and under surfaces in seemingly unexplainable ways. And of course, we would have to get the stain out. Our task would be difficult as nearly every exposed surface (save the yellow walls) had recently been painted white.

With such a daunting task before us, we first paused to observe the mayhem. One could not have painted a better picture intentionally. The explosion moved and dissipated from the inside out in a perfect gradient. You almost wish it had been intentional, but it had not been. So, with a sigh, we set to work and began to clean the thick, red paste off of each surface and crevice (save, of course, those spaces we didn't even conceive to look in. I mean, who looks under a cupboard for something that hit the ceiling and exploded from above the counter? We found that months later).

Of course, the kitchen does not look like this now. No, the kitchen has been repainted at least twice since then. Not because of the tomato sauce explosion, mind you, but simply because the kitchen was not fit to the cook's liking. And, maybe also to cover up similar kitchen mistakes. The walls are white now, the cupboards are too, and there are now more surfaces onto which various experiments have made their way.

Many things look different about this room, and I am always wondering what will have changed each time I enter the lab of bakers and cooks: the Kitchen. There is little wonder why technicians and scientists have stolen the name. They too have long since left behind the evidence of their presence and inventions around their workspace. But even after all these years, whenever I enter that space in the center of my old home, I can't help but glance up at the ceiling and see if I can find the remaining evidence of one of my mother's first attempts at canning tomato sauce. And maybe it's a trick of the eye, but I think I still can, and I am glad for the memory.

BBQ Sauce

Ingredients:

- 1 cup brown sugar
- ¼ cup Worcestershire sauce
- ¼ cup apple cider vinegar
- ¼ cup chili sauce
- ½ cup ketchup
- ⅓ cup soy sauce
- 2 tsp prepared mustard
- 2 cloves garlic, minced
- ⅛ tsp pepper

Instructions:

1. Mix all ingredients in a small bowl.
2. Keep refrigerated until use.

Everything Sauce

Ingredients:

- ⅓ cup mayonnaise
- 2 tbls Dijon mustard
- 2 tbls barbecue sauce
- ½ tbl honey
- ½ tbl Worcestershire sauce
- ¼ tsp lemon juice
- ⅛ tsp paprika
- ¼ tsp salt
- ½ tsp garlic powder

Instructions:

1. Mix all ingredients in a small bowl.
2. Keep refrigerated until use.

Cheese Sauce

Ingredients:

- 2 ½ tbls butter
- ½ tbl flour
- ¾ cup milk
- 2 cups fresh shredded cheddar cheese
- ½ tsp chili powder
- ¼ tsp salt

Instructions:

1. Melt butter and flour in a small saucepan until it starts to bubble, whisking continually.
2. Whisk in milk and let the mixture thicken for 2 minutes. Turn off the heat. Do not let it overheat or it will be too thick.
3. Add cheese and seasoning, stirring together as it melts.
4. If the sauce is too thick, add in milk by the tablespoon and adjust the seasoning to taste.

Ranch Dressing

Ingredients:

- ¼ cup buttermilk
- 1 cup sour cream
- ¾ tsp onion powder
- ½ tsp garlic powder
- ½ tsp dried chives
- ½ tsp dried dill
- ½ tsp dried parsley
- ¼ tsp salt
- pinch of black pepper

Instructions:

1. Whisk together all ingredients in a small bowl.
2. Refrigerate for 1 hour before serving.

Apple Filling

Cook Time: 15 min.

Ingredients:

- 3 medium apples (2 ½ cups diced)
- 2 tbls butter
- ⅓ cup sugar
- 3 tbls water
- 1 tsp ground cinnamon
- 1 tbl flour

Instructions:

1. Wash, core, and dice apples.
2. Pulse apples in a food processor until finely chopped, but not fully pureed.
3. Melt butter in a medium saucepan over a medium heat and add sugar, water, cinnamon, and flour.
4. Add apples and heat for 15 minutes, stirring continuously.
5. Remove from heat and cool in a small bowl.
6. Scrape the filling into a pastry bag, or freeze it in a freezer bag for long-term storage.

Blueberry Filling

Cook Time: 10 min.

Ingredients:

- 4 cups blueberries
- 1 tsp lemon juice
- ½ cup sugar
- ½ tsp ground cinnamon
- ¼ tsp ground nutmeg
- 2 tbls cornstarch
- 3 tbls water
- 2 tbls butter

Instructions:

1. When making a pie filling, blend 1 cup of blueberries in a pastry blender. If making a pastry filling, puree all of the blueberries.
2. Combine blueberries with lemon juice, sugar, and spices.
3. Stir cornstarch and water in a small bowl.
4. Melt butter in a medium saucepan and add all ingredients.
5. Bring to a medium heat, stirring continually for 5 minutes.
6. Once the filling begins to bubble, simmer for 1 minute and quickly remove from heat. Scrape the filling into a medium bowl to cool.
7. Scrape filling into a pastry bag, pie crust, or freezer bag for long-term storage.

Lemon Filling

Cook Time: 10 min.

Ingredients:

- 1 ¼ cups sugar
- 6 tbls cornstarch
- ⅔ cup lemon juice
- 4 egg yolks
- 1 ½ cups water, boiling
- 2 tbls butter

Instructions:

1. In a medium saucepan, whisk together sugar, cornstarch, and lemon juice.
2. Beat egg yolks in a small bowl. Whisk into lemon mixture.
3. Turn heat to medium and, while constantly stirring, gradually add in water.
4. Stir for 6-8 minutes until the mixture boils and thickens.
5. Remove from heat and stir in butter.
6. Add to your dish or cool, scrape into a piping bag, and add to your pastry of choice.

Vanilla Custard Filling

Cook Time: 10 min.

Ingredients:

- 1 cup milk
- 4 tsp cornstarch
- ¼ cup sugar
- 1 egg yolk, beaten
- 1 ½ tsp vanilla extract

Instructions:

1. In a small saucepan, dissolve cornstarch into milk.
2. Heat the saucepan to medium-high and add sugar, egg yolk, and vanilla.
3. Whisk ingredients continually and bring to a boil.
4. Continue stirring for another 2-3 minutes.
5. Remove from heat and set aside to thicken and cool. You can also spread the custard onto a flat dish to cool more quickly.
6. Once cool, add to your dish of choice or scoop into a piping bag for pastry filling.

Vanilla Cream Filling

Cook Time: 2 ½ hrs.

Ingredients:

- 2 cups milk
- 2 tsp vanilla extract
- ½ cup sugar
- 3 egg yolks, beaten
- 3 tbls cornstarch
- ⅛ tsp salt
- ½ cup heavy cream

Instructions:

1. Bring milk and vanilla to a boil in a medium saucepan. As soon as it reaches a boil, turn off the heat.
2. Beat egg yolks and sugar in a small bowl. Stir in cornstarch and salt and whisk for 5 minutes.
3. Take ½ cup of the hot milk and whisk into the egg mixture.
4. Add the egg mixture to the milk and whisk together.
5. Bring to a boil and whisk for 5 minutes.
6. Pour into a medium bowl through a mesh strainer.
7. Cover the custard with plastic wrap, laying the wrap onto the surface.
8. Refrigerate for 2 hours.
9. Whip heavy cream to stiff peaks and fold into the custard.
10. Spoon into a tipped pastry bag for filling your pastry of choice.

Raspberry Picking

The two explorers set out on their mission. Objective: raspberry jam. They packed a little basket, put on their shoes, and headed for the great outdoors. First, they would have to pass the pond and not get stopped by the peach tree. But there at the end of the journey was their treasure: the raspberry patch.

Honestly, it was not that far of a hike. Just a trip from the back door to the stretch of garden behind the garage. But what a find! Raspberries everywhere! There were red raspberries, pink raspberries, white unripe raspberries, deep overripe raspberries, and the favorites (because they *definitely* tasted different): golden raspberries.

Together, the two young adventurers picked as many raspberries as they could find. Well, as many raspberries as they had the patience for, which was about a third of the basket. Their guide, a friend making sure they didn't get into too much mischief, stood back watching. She agreed they had enough to make at least a little jam, so off they went, returning through the high grass and steep steps back to the kitchen.

One adventurer mashed the raspberries while the other got sugar. Well, she couldn't find the sugar, so applesauce it was. Mixing the two ingredients together proved a delicious treat, and they ate it straight from the bowl before it made its way to any toast. The guide smiled, knowing that, though sweet, such a treat was a far cry from jam. But to the two adventures, it was mashed raspberries, just like their mom made. So, what was the real difference? And their creation tasted good, and that was all that mattered.

Breads, Biscuits, and Baked Goods

Amish White Bread

Temp: 350°F   **Cook Time:** 30 min.

Ingredients:

- 1 cup water, warm
- 1 cup milk, warm
- 1 tbl-⅔ cup sugar or honey
- 2 ½ tsp yeast
- ¼ cup olive oil or melted butter
- 5 ½-6 cups flour
- 1 tsp salt

Instructions:

1. In a mixing bowl, combine water, milk, yeast, and sugar. More sugar will make a sweeter and denser bread for French toast or jam. Less sugar is better for sandwiches.
2. Proof yeast for 10 minutes.
3. Mix in oil, salt, and 5 ½ cups flour. Slowly add more flour until the dough is tacky but soft.
4. Knead for 10 minutes to form an elastic dough.
5. Cover and rise for 1 hour in a warm place until the dough has doubled. Then punch down dough and divide it in half.
6. Roll out each dough portion into a rectangle and roll into a loaf, folding under the ends.
7. Place rolls into two greased 9x5" bread pans.
8. Cover and rise for 30 minutes, or until the dough has doubled.
9. Preheat oven to 350°F.
10. Bake in the oven for 30 minutes.
11. Remove from oven, brush with butter, and cool before cutting.

Cinnamon Egg Bread

Temp: 350°F   **Cook Time:** 30 min.

Ingredients:

- ⅓ cup sugar
- 3 tsp yeast
- 1 ½ cup milk, warm
- ½ cup butter, melted
- 1 tsp vanilla extract
- 4 eggs, beaten
- ½ tsp salt
- 5 ½-6 ½ cups flour

Filling

- ⅔ cup sugar
- 1 ½ tbls ground cinnamon

Instructions:

1. In a mixing bowl, proof yeast in warm milk and sugar for 10 minutes.
2. Mix in butter, vanilla, eggs, and salt.
3. Slowly add in flour until the dough forms a non-sticky ball.
4. Knead in a stand mixer for 10 minutes and then on a floured surface for another 5 minutes to form an elastic dough.
5. Cover with a cloth and rise for 1 hour.
6. Punch down the dough and roll it out into a large, ¼" thick rectangle.
7. Cover evenly with cinnamon sugar filling.
8. Roll the dough into a log, cut it in half, and pinch the ends.
9. Place dough logs into two greased 9x5" bread pans.
10. Rise for 30-60 minutes or until the dough has doubled.
11. Preheat oven to 350°F.
12. Bake in the oven for 30 minutes.
13. Let the bread cool before cutting.

Cracked Wheat Bread

Temp: 325°F

Cook Time: 50 min.

Ingredients:

- 6 tbls water, warm
- 2 ¼ tsp yeast
- ¼ cup cracked wheat
- 1 tbl flax seed, ground
- 1 tbl sunflower seeds, chopped
- ¼ cup walnuts, chopped

- ½ cup water, warm
- ½ cup buttermilk
- 2 tbls honey
- 2 tbls olive oil
- 1 ¾ cups whole wheat flour
- ½ cup flour
- 1 tsp salt

Instructions:

1. Dissolve yeast in 6 tbls of warm water until frothy.
2. Soak cracked wheat, flax seed, sunflower seeds, and walnuts in water, buttermilk, honey, and olive oil for 10 minutes.
3. Mix flours and salt in a large mixing bowl with other ingredients. Knead for 10 minutes.
4. Place in a greased bowl and cover with a warm, damp cloth.
5. Set in a warm place to rise for 2 ½ hours.
6. Punch down and rise for another 1 ½ hours.
7. Punch down and rest for another 10 minutes.
8. Form into a loaf and place in a greased 9x5" bread pan.
9. Rise for 1 hour or until the dough is 1" above the pan.
10. Preheat oven to 325°F.
11. Bake for 50 minutes.
12. Take it out of the oven and wait 10 minutes before removing the bread from the pan. Brush with butter, cut, and serve.

Oatmeal Bread

Temp: 325°F   **Cook Time:** 50 min.

Ingredients:

- 6 tbls water, warm
- 2 ¼ tsp yeast
- 1 cup rolled oats
- ½ cup water, warm
- ½ cup buttermilk
- 2 tbls honey
- 2 tbls olive oil
- ½ cup whole wheat flour
- 1 ½ cups flour
- 1 tsp salt

Instructions:

1. Dissolve yeast in 6 tbls of warm water until frothy.
2. Soak oats in water, buttermilk, honey, and olive oil for 10 minutes.
3. Mix flours and salt in a large mixing bowl with other ingredients.
4. Knead for 10 minutes.
5. Place in a greased bowl and cover with a warm, damp cloth.
6. Set in a warm place to rise for 2 ½ hours.
7. Punch down and let rise for another 1 ½ hours.
8. Punch down and rest for another 10 minutes.
9. Form into a loaf and place in a greased 9x5" bread pan.
10. Rise for 1 hour or until the dough is 1" above the pan.
11. Preheat oven to 325°F.
12. Bake for 50 minutes.
13. Take it out of the oven and wait 10 minutes before removing the bread from the pan. Brush with butter, cut, and serve.

Whole Wheat Raisin Bread

Temp: 325°F

Cook Time: 50 min.

Ingredients:

- 6 tbls water, warm
- 2 ¼ tsp yeast
- ½ cup raisins
- ⅓ cup walnuts, chopped
- ½ cup water
- ½ cup buttermilk
- ¼ cup honey
- 2 tbls olive oil
- 1 ¾ cups whole wheat flour
- 1 cup white flour
- 1 tsp salt

Filling

- 2 tbls ground cinnamon
- 2 tbls sugar

Instructions:

1. Proof yeast in warm water for 10 minutes.
2. Soak raisins and walnuts in water, buttermilk, honey, and olive oil for 10 minutes.
3. Mix flours and salt in a large mixing bowl with other ingredients. Knead for 10 minutes.
4. Place in a greased bowl and cover with a warm, damp cloth.
5. Set in a warm place to rise for 2 ½ hours.
6. Punch down and rise for another 1 ½ hours.
7. Punch down and rest for another 10 minutes.
8. Mix cinnamon and sugar. Roll out dough into a large rectangle and sprinkle with cinnamon sugar mixture.
9. Roll into a loaf and set in a greased 9x5" bread pan.
10. Rise for 1 hour or until the dough is 1" above the pan.
11. Preheat oven to 325°F and bake bread for 50 minutes.
12. Take it out of the oven and wait 10 minutes before removing the bread from the pan. Brush with butter, cut, and serve.

Morning Coffee

A quiet buzzing woke Eddy from the opposite side of the house. He turned to his right. Five o'clock. Time to start the day. Shuffling from his bed, he found a robe and began walking down the short hall to the kitchen to stop the insistent sound. With the last buzz cut short, the house was quiet. The early light was just peeking through the overgrown trees and foggy windows, making the morning seem not here but a handful of states away. The smell of coffee and smoke brought him back.

His favorite mug was already on the counter and as he began to pour, he noticed another smaller cup beside it. Pausing, he looked behind him and noticed the sleepy tousled head that found herself at the kitchen table with bright anticipation. He smiled — if one could call the slight rising of the lips a smile — and got the milk and sugar out too. No need to start a caffeine habit this early.

Together, they sipped their coffee and coffee-flavored sugar-milk, happily enjoying the sunrise. Quiet, and content. He had forgotten this morning tradition yesterday. Well, not exactly. He had to leave early, and Joey woke up late. Her sister brought the younger's lamentations to him when Joey complained that her coffee simply was not the same with anyone else. He smiled again.

As they finished the last sip and placed their mugs side by side in the sink, Joey smiled and hugged him. He patted her head and they both moved on to the day's tasks of work and school. The morning was over, and the day had begun. And though they would be parted during the day in this winter weather, Eddy knew he might smile again thinking back to this warm morning together.

Cheesy Drop Biscuits

Temp: 425°F   **Cook Time:** 14 min.

Ingredients:

- 2 cups flour
- 2 ½ tsp baking powder
- ½ tsp baking soda
- 1 tbl sugar
- 1 tsp salt
- 1 tsp garlic powder (optional)
- 1 ½ cups cheddar cheese, shredded (optional)
- ½ cup butter, melted and cooled
- 1 cup buttermilk

Topping

- ¼ cup butter, melted
- 1 tsp parsley
- ½ tsp garlic powder
- ¼ tsp salt

Instructions:

1. Preheat oven to 425°F.
2. Mix all the dry ingredients in a medium bowl.
3. Whisk the butter into the milk and add to the dry ingredients.
4. Using either a large cookie scoop or a spoon, drop twenty-four mounds of batter onto two parchment-lined baking sheets.
5. Place sheets into the oven and bake for 14 minutes or until golden. Rotate sheets halfway through.
6. Remove from oven and brush with topping mixture, if desired, and serve.

Cornbread

Temp: 400°F   **Cook Time:** 20-25 min.

Ingredients:

- 1 cup flour
- 2 cups cornmeal
- 1 tsp salt
- 3 tsp baking powder
- ½ tsp baking soda
- ⅓ cup sugar
- ¼ cup brown sugar
- 4 tbls butter, softened
- 3 eggs, beaten
- 1 cup buttermilk
- 15 oz. cream corn

Instructions:

1. Preheat oven to 400°F.
2. In a medium bowl, whisk together flour, cornmeal, salt, baking powder, and baking soda.
3. In a large bowl, mix sugar with the softened butter. Then mix in eggs, buttermilk, and cream corn.
4. Add the dry ingredients to the wet ingredients and stir until just combined.
5. Butter a 12" cast-iron pan or grease a 9x13" baking dish and pour in batter.
6. Place pan in the oven and cook for 20-25 minutes until the center is firm.
7. Remove from oven and serve warm.

Dinner Rolls

Temp: 360°F

Cook Time: 15-20 min.

Ingredients:

- 1 tbl instant yeast
- ¼ cup sugar
- 1 ½ cups milk, warm
- 4 tbls butter, melted
- 1 tsp salt
- 1 egg, beaten
- 4 ½ cups (bread) flour

- 3 tbls butter, melted

Instructions:

1. In a large bowl or stand mixer, dissolve yeast and sugar in warm milk.
2. Add in butter, salt, and egg.
3. Slowly mix in flour and knead for 10 minutes. The result should be a soft dough that is not too sticky.
4. Cover dough, set in a warm place, and rise for 1 hour until doubled.
5. Scrape onto the counter, divide the dough into 15 portions, and roll into balls.
6. Place rolls into a greased 9x13" baking dish.
7. Let them rise for 20 minutes, or until they have doubled.
8. Preheat oven to 360°F.
9. After the rolls have risen, bake them for 15-20 minutes, or until the tops are golden.
10. Melt about 3 tbls of butter in a small dish.
11. Remove rolls from the oven and brush with melted butter.
12. Cut and serve with jam or butter.

Chałka

Temp: 350°F

Cook Time: 30 min.

Ingredients:

- 1 cup milk
- ½ cup butter, softened
- 5 tsp instant yeast
- ¼ cup water, warm
- ¾ cup sugar
- 3 eggs, beaten

- 1 tsp salt
- 5 ½-6 cups flour
- 1 cup raisins (optional)

- 1 egg
- 1 tbl milk

Instructions:

1. In a small saucepan, bring milk and butter to a simmer. Let it simmer for 1 minute then set it aside to cool.
2. Proof yeast in water in a large mixing bowl for 10 minutes.
3. Add cooled milk to the yeast and beat in eggs and sugar.
4. Add salt and mix in flour one cup at a time. Knead for 10 minutes. It should form a soft, elastic dough ball.
5. Place dough in a greased bowl, cover, and set in a warm place to rise for 1 hour, or until doubled.
6. Punch down dough and divide it in half and divide the halves into thirds.
7. Braid dough, pinch under ends, and set on a parchment-lined baking pan.
8. Cover and rise again for 35 minutes.
9. Preheat oven to 350°F.
10. Mix egg with milk and brush over the braided loaves.
11. Place in oven and bake for 30 minutes, or until golden.
12. Remove from oven and cool for 10 minutes before serving.

French Bread

Temp: 450°F   **Cook Time:** 25 min.

Ingredients:

- 1 ½ cups water, warm
- 1 tbl honey
- 2 tsp salt
- 3 ½-4 cups flour
- 2 tsp instant yeast
- olive oil
- 1 egg (optional)

Instructions:

1. Stir water, yeast, and honey in a mixing bowl. Let it sit for 5 minutes.
2. Add salt and knead in 3 cups of flour. If the dough is still sticky, slowly add flour to form a soft, elastic dough.
3. Form dough into a ball, brush with olive oil, cover, and let it rise for 30 minutes.
4. Stretch (don't rip) and fold dough four times, once on each side. Cover and rise for 30 minutes. Repeat this three times.
5. After the last rise, you can start with step 6, rise for another 3 hours, or let it rise for twelve hours in the refrigerator.
6. Set the dough on a floured surface and cut it in half. Roll each half into a rectangle and tightly roll into a 16" loaf. Tuck ends underneath the loaf on each side.
7. Place on a parchment-lined pan or a baguette pan and rise for another 40 minutes until they are puffy but not doubled.
8. Preheat oven to 450°F. Set a metal dish on the bottom rack.
9. Cut five lines on the tops of loaves, place them in the oven, and pour ½ cup of water into the metal baking dish below.
10. Bake loaves for 25 minutes, or until they are golden brown. If desired, brush a beaten egg onto the loaves after 12 minutes.
11. Remove and cool for 10 minutes before serving.

Olive Oil Dough

Ingredients:

- 1 ½ tbls yeast
- 1 tbl sugar
- 2 ¾ cups water, warm
- ¼ cup olive oil
- 1 ½ tsp salt
- 6 ½ cups flour

Instructions:

1. Add yeast and sugar to a large mixing bowl.
2. Add warm water and proof yeast for 10 minutes.
3. Add olive oil and salt to the bowl and stir together.
4. Turn on the stand mixer and add flour one cup at a time.
5. Once all the flour is added, continue mixing for 10 minutes.
6. Remove the soft dough ball and place it in a larger greased bowl. Cover with a warm damp towel, and place in a warm spot to rise for 1 hour.

There are multiple dishes you can make with this recipe:

Bread

1) Punch down the dough and divide it in two.
2) Form into loaves and either place them on an oiled baking pan or place them in two well-oiled cast-iron pans.
3) If desired, brush with olive oil and add toppings of choice.
4) Preheat oven to 375°F and let the loaves rise for 35 minutes.
5) Place loaves in the oven and bake for 30 minutes.
6) Remove from oven, cool, and serve. If desired, brush with butter and top with parmesan.

Pizza

1) After the dough has risen once, punch down and preheat the oven to 475°F with two pizza stones or cast-iron pans.
2) Separate the dough into three parts. Save ⅓ for breadsticks. Stretch out two dough pieces to a ½" thick 12" circle.
3) Remove pans from the oven carefully and set on the stovetop.
4) Place the dough onto a heated and oiled pizza stone or cast-iron pan.
5) Add pizza sauce, leaving 1" for the crust.
6) Add cheese, covering evenly and onto the space not covered by the sauce. Add other toppings of choice.
7) Bake pizzas for 15 minutes, or until the cheese turns golden.
8) Remove from oven and brush crust with butter and parmesan.

Cinnamon or Parmesan Breadsticks

1) Take ⅓ of the dough and roll it out to a ½" thick rectangle.
2) Place on a greased baking sheet and preheat oven to 400°F.
3) Mix ½ cup brown sugar, 1 tbl flour, and 2 tsp cinnamon.
   a. *Or* ⅓ cup melted butter and ⅓ cup parmesan cheese.
4) Coat the dough evenly with topping. Bake for 20 minutes.

Pizza Rolls

1) Preheat oven to 400°F and cut dough into 8 pieces.
2) Roll out into 8x8" squares.
3) Spoon 3 tbls of pizza sauce onto each and spread evenly, but not to the edges. Top with 2 tbls mozzarella cheese and an ounce of pepperoni slices or sausage chunks.
4) Roll tightly, pinch off the edges, and brush with butter.
5) Place on a greased baking sheet and bake for 30 minutes.

Pita Bread

Cook Time: 35 min.

Ingredients:

- 4 tsp yeast
- 1 cup milk, warm
- 1 ⅓ cups water, warm
- 2 tsp sugar
- 2 tsp salt
- 2 tbls olive oil
- 6 cups flour
- olive oil

Instructions:

1. Proof yeast in warm water and milk in a large mixing bowl.
2. After 10 minutes, add in the sugar, salt, and olive oil.
3. Mix in flour and knead for 6 minutes to form a smooth dough.
4. Set the dough in a warm place to rise for 30 minutes.
5. Divide dough into 16 balls and let them rest for 15 minutes.
6. Get either a fry pan or cast-iron pan and heat to a medium-low heat.
7. Using either your hands (softer pita) or a rolling pin (firmer pita), shape the dough on a floured surface into 8" circles.
8. Pour a dash of olive oil into the pan or cast-iron pan to coat in a thin layer.
9. Bake each side for 2-3 minutes. For a softer pita, place a lid ajar on the pan to steam.
10. Remove from pan and cool before storing or serve immediately.

Pizza Dough

Temp: 500°F   **Cook Time:** 12-15 min.

Ingredients:

- 1 ⅔ cups water, warm
- 2 tsp yeast
- 1 tbl olive oil

- 2 tsp salt
- 1 tsp sugar
- 4 ¼ cups (bread) flour

Instructions:

1. Proof yeast for 10 minutes and add olive oil, salt, and sugar.
2. Mix in 4 cups flour. The dough will be tacky and soft. If needed, add the remaining flour.
3. Knead for 5 minutes until you have an elastic dough. Set it in a large bowl and cover it with a lid or kitchen towel.
4. Set in the refrigerator for 24 hours and set out 2 hours before moving to the next steps or set in a warm place for 2-8 hours.
5. Preheat oven to 500°F. If using, put cast-iron pans in oven.
6. Remove the dough from the bowl and divide it in half.
7. Stretch dough into pizza rounds on flour or tossed with your hands, starting from the center. You want a rounded, undisturbed edge of dough for the crust.
8. If using, take the cast iron out of the oven and pour enough olive oil onto them to coat the bottom. Or brush pans with oil.
9. Set the dough onto pans or cast iron and brush the top of the dough generously with olive oil. Rest for 10 minutes.
10. Add sauce and toppings onto the dough, leaving a 1-2" edge.
11. Place one pan at a time in the oven for 12-15 minutes or until the cheese is golden.
12. Remove from oven and cool. If desired, brush butter onto the crust and dust with garlic salt and parmesan cheese.

Tortillas

Cook Time: 15 min.

Ingredients:

- 3 cups flour
- 1 tsp salt
- ½ tsp baking powder
- ¼ cup olive oil, butter, or lard
- 1 cup water

Instructions:

1. Mix all ingredients and knead for 5 minutes.
2. Wrap and set the dough aside for 30 minutes.
3. Divide the dough into 6-12 portions. The more portions, the smaller the tortillas will be.
4. Roll each portion on a floured surface into a 6"-12" circle.
5. Heat a large fry pan to a medium heat and bake each tortilla for 30 seconds on each side.
6. Set in a warm place on a kitchen towel until ready to serve.

Banana Bread

Temp: 350°F   **Cook Time:** 1 hr. 15 min.

Ingredients:

- 4 cups mashed bananas (6-8 bananas)
- 1 ½ cups butter, softened
- 1 cup sour cream
- 5 eggs, beaten
- 5 cups flour
- 2 cups sugar
- 2 tsp baking powder
- 2 tsp baking soda
- 2 cups walnuts, chopped

Instructions:

1. Preheat oven to 325°F and grease three 9x5" bread pans.
2. Mash bananas in a large bowl and mix in wet ingredients.
3. In a separate bowl, mix dry ingredients.
4. Mix dry ingredients into wet ingredients until just combined. Do not over-mix.
5. Pour batter into the three bread pans.
6. Bake for 1 hour and check to see if the center of fully done with a toothpick. If it is not done, bake for another fifteen minutes and check again.
7. Let the bread cool for 10 minutes before removing it from the pan to cut and serve.

Beer Bread

Temp: 350°F   **Cook Time:** 50 min.

Ingredients:

- 3 cups flour
- ½ cup sugar
- 1 ½ tbls baking powder
- 1 tsp salt
- 12 oz. (1 ½ cups) beer or soda, room temp
- ¼ cup butter, melted
- ½ tbl ground cinnamon (optional)
- 1 tsp vanilla extract (optional)

Instructions:

1. Preheat oven to 350°F.
2. Mix dry ingredients in a medium bowl.
3. Mix in wet ingredients until just combined.
4. Pour into a greased 9x5" bread pan.
5. Cook for 50 minutes.
6. Remove from oven and cool for 10 minutes in pan.
7. Remove from pan, cut, and serve with jam or butter.

Pumpkin Bread

Temp: 325°F   **Cook Time:** 1 hr. 15 min.

Ingredients:

- 1 ¾ cups flour
- ½ tsp salt
- 1 tsp baking soda
- ½ tsp baking powder
- ½ tsp ground cloves
- 1 tsp ground cinnamon
- ¼ tsp ground nutmeg
- ¾ cup butter, softened
- 1 cup sugar
- ½ cup brown sugar
- 2 eggs, beaten

- 2 tsp vanilla extract
- 15 oz. pure pumpkin
- ½ cup milk
- ⅔ cup chocolate chips (optional)

Topping

- ½ cup flour
- ¼ cup brown sugar
- 2 tbls sugar
- ½ tsp pie spice
- ½ cup butter, softened

Instructions:

1. Preheat oven to 325°F.
2. Whisk together dry ingredients in a medium bowl.
3. In a large bowl, cream butter and sugars. Beat in eggs.
4. Add vanilla and beat in pumpkin and milk.
5. Add the flour mixture to the wet ingredients and mix until just combined. If desired, add chocolate chips.
6. Grease two 9x5" pans and divide the batter between them.
7. Take the dry ingredients bowl and mix the topping ingredients, cutting in the butter to form a crumbly texture.
8. Add the crumble topping to each pan evenly.
9. Place pans in the oven and bake for 1 hour and 15 minutes.
10. When a toothpick comes clean from the bread, remove the bread from the oven, cool, and serve.

Zucchini Bread

Temp: 350°F   **Cook Time:** 45-60 min.

Ingredients:

- 3 eggs, beaten
- 1 ½ cups sugar, or honey
- ¾ cup butter, melted
- 1 cup grated zucchini
- 3 cups flour
- 1 cup raisins or chocolate chips
- 1 tsp salt
- 1 tsp baking soda
- 1-2 tsp ground cinnamon
- ¼ tsp baking powder
- 1 tsp vanilla extract
- 1 cup walnuts, chopped

Instructions:

1. Preheat oven to 350°F.
2. Beat eggs until foamy.
3. Stir in the wet ingredients into the eggs.
4. In a separate bowl, whisk together dry ingredients. Then mix the dry ingredients into the wet ingredients.
5. Pour batter into two buttered and floured 9x5" bread pans.
6. Bake for 45-60 minutes.
7. Remove from oven and cool for 10 minutes.
8. After the bread has cooled, remove from pans, cut, and serve.

Double Chocolate Zucchini Bread

Temp: 350°F   **Cook Time:** 40-45 min.

Ingredients:

- 1 cup sugar
- 1 cup brown sugar
- 1 cup butter, softened
- ½ cup sour cream
- 4 eggs, beaten
- 1 cup buttermilk
- 1 tsp vanilla extract
- 4 cups flour

- 3 tsp baking soda
- 1 tsp salt
- 1 tsp ground cinnamon
- 7 tbls cocoa powder
- 4 cups zucchini, shredded
- 12 oz. mini chocolate chips

Instructions:

1. Preheat oven to 350°F.
2. Cream sugars with the butter and then stir in sour cream, eggs, buttermilk, and vanilla.
3. In a separate bowl, whisk together dry ingredients. Then mix the dry ingredients into the wet ingredients.
4. Pour batter into two greased 9x5" bread pans or four mini loaf pans.
5. Bake for 40-45 minutes or until the centers are set.
6. Remove from oven and cool for 10 minutes.
7. After the bread has cooled, remove from pans, cut, and serve.

"It's just OK."

It is a truth universally acknowledged that one does not comment negatively on a cook's cooking in-house. Scenes from movies may flash before your eyes at such a thought. A particularly snobbish patron decides to make a scene at the lack of creativity on the cook's part. And the cook, wanting to defend his good name and delightful dish, responds in no uncertain terms, regardless of the truth of the claim.

But such scenes rarely resulted in equal intensity growing up. If you did not like something, the answer was, "I'm not a short-order cook." End of conversation. There were many things I and my siblings did not like, including stir-fry, BBQ sauce, any sort of meat that was not chicken, and cucumbers (I'll leave you to decide who didn't like what). We endured or starved. But somewhere along the way, I think the cook in our house forgot that some people *really* do not like certain things.

And thus came the night when my husband and I came over for dinner. What were we eating? Was it stuffed cabbages, soup, a pasta dish? I honestly cannot remember. But, dear reader, it was a dish with one flaw: it had onions. Now, my husband hates onions, and this cook loved them. But, as a sort of experiment, she decided to sneak them in unawares.

The table was set, the dishes were served, and everyone ate happily, munching between bits of chatter and laughter. It was smooth sailing until the cook asked the fated question.

"What do you think of the meal?"

He paused, and responded honestly, "It's just OK."

The room, for one moment, sat in silent horror as the words everyone had, at one time or another, thought, but never spoken. Those words that caused no words and, in that moment, would have allowed for the ticking of the clock to be heard if the clock had (ever) worked. They sat and stared, but only for a moment, as the cook had the words to say.

"Just 'OK'? No one calls my cooking OK!"

"Yeah, it was just OK. Not bad, but not my favorite."

A loud, exasperated sigh escaped the cook. "How did you know?" she demanded.

"Know what?" he asked.

"Know that I put onions in it!"

"Oh! So that's what it was."

"You can't even taste them!"

Dubious, he looked at the cook. "Then why did you put them in?"

The guests again looked at each other, and burst out laughing, as each knew of at least one time a particular ingredient was added in hopes that we would not notice. The tiny cucumber slices, the cauliflower in exchange for potatoes, or the meat that was definitely different from the last time it was named thus. So, we laughed again. For in truth, it was a good meal. And in truth, no one's feelings were seriously hurt. For in truth, you will always get a truthful answer if you ask it from someone who cares.

Scones

Temp: 400°F   **Cook Time:** 20 min.

Ingredients:

- 3 cups flour
- 1 tbl baking powder
- ½ cup sugar
- ½ tsp salt
- ½ cup butter, cold
- ⅔ cup dried cranberries
- 2 ¼ cups heavy cream
- 2 tsp vanilla extract
- milk
- sugar

Instructions:

1. Preheat oven to 400°F.
2. Combine flour, sugar, baking powder, and salt.
3. Using a pastry blender, cut in butter until it is in grain-sized pieces.
4. Add dried cranberries, heavy cream, and vanilla, mixing until just combined.
5. Divide dough and pat into two 8" circles on a parchment-lined baking sheet and cut them into 8 wedges.
   a. Alternatively, scoop dough into a greased 12-cup muffin pan. It should make between 18-24 muffins.
6. Brush scones with milk and dust with sugar.
7. Bake for 20 minutes or until golden.
8. Remove from oven and serve warm.

Banana Muffins

Temp: 425°F; 350°F   **Cook Time:** 20 mins.

Ingredients:

- 2 cups mashed bananas (3-4 bananas)
- ¼ cup sugar
- ¾ cup brown sugar
- ½ cup butter, softened
- 1½ tsp vanilla extract
- ½ cup buttermilk
- 2 eggs, beaten

- 2 ¼ cups flour
- 1 tsp baking soda
- 2 tsp baking powder
- ½ tsp salt
- 1½ tsp ground cinnamon
- 1 cup chocolate chips

Instructions:

1. Preheat oven to 425°F and grease a mini bread pan and a 12-cup muffin pan.
2. Mash bananas in a large bowl and mix in wet ingredients.
3. In a separate bowl, mix dry ingredients.
4. Mix dry ingredients into wet ingredients until just combined. Do not over-mix the batter.
5. Fill the muffin pan cups until the cups are almost full. Pour the remaining batter into the mini loaf pan.
6. Bake for 7 minutes at 425°F and then for another 13 minutes at 350°F.
   a. Mini muffins should bake at 375 for 15 minutes.
   b. A 9x5" bread pan should bake for 10 minutes at 425°F and then for another 40 minutes at 350°F.
7. When the centers are springy, remove muffins from the oven.
8. Cool for 10 minutes before removing muffins or bread from the pan.

Blueberry Muffins

Temp: 425°F; 375°F   **Cook Time:** 20 min.

Ingredients:

- ½ cup butter, melted
- ⅔ cup milk
- 2 eggs, beaten
- 1 tsp vanilla extract
- 1 cup sugar
- 2 cups flour
- 1 tsp baking soda

- 3 tsp baking powder
- ½ tsp salt
- 1 cup blueberries

Topping

- ⅓ cup flour
- ⅓ cup brown sugar
- ¼ cup butter, softened

Instructions:

1. Preheat oven to 425°F.
2. Melt butter in a large mixing bowl and mix in milk, eggs, vanilla, and sugar.
3. In a separate smaller bowl, mix flour, baking soda, baking powder, and salt.
4. Add dry ingredients to wet ingredients, add blueberries, and mix until just combined.
5. Line a 12-cup muffin pan with muffin papers or coat in cooking spray. Fill each muffin cup ¾ full.
6. In the smaller bowl, blend flour, brown sugar, and butter for the muffin topping. Sprinkle the topping on the muffins.
7. Place pans in the oven and bake for 7 minutes at 425°F and then for another 13 minutes at 350°F.
8. Remove from oven when centers are springy.
9. Cool for a few minutes, then remove from pans and serve.

Chocolate Muffins

Temp: 425°F; 375°F

Cook Time: 20 min.

Ingredients:

- ½ cup butter, melted
- ½ cup milk
- 2 eggs, beaten
- ¼ cup sour cream
- 1 tsp vanilla extract
- 1 cup sugar
- 1 ¾ cups flour
- ½ cup cocoa powder
- 1 tsp baking soda
- 2 tsp baking powder
- ½ tsp salt
- 1 ½ cups chocolate chunks

Instructions:

1. Preheat oven to 425°F.
2. Melt butter in a large mixing bowl and mix in milk, eggs, sour cream, vanilla, and sugar.
3. In a separate smaller bowl, mix flour, cocoa, baking soda, baking powder, salt, and chocolate chunks.
4. Add dry ingredients to wet ingredients and mix until just combined.
5. Line a 12-cup muffin pan with muffin papers or coat in cooking spray. Fill each muffin cup ¾ full.
6. Place pans in the oven and bake for 7 minutes at 425°F and then for another 13 minutes at 350°F.
7. Remove from oven when centers are springy.
8. Cool for a few minutes, then remove from pans and serve.

Chocolate Chip Muffins

Temp: 425°F; 375°F   **Cook Time:** 20 min.

Ingredients:

- ½ cup butter, melted
- ¾ cup milk
- 2 eggs, beaten
- 2 tsp vanilla extract
- 1 cup sugar
- 2 cups flour
- 1 tsp baking soda
- 3 tsp baking powder
- ½ tsp salt
- 1 ½ cups chocolate chips

Instructions:

1. Preheat oven to 425°F.
2. Melt butter in a large mixing bowl and mix in milk, eggs, vanilla, and sugar.
3. In a separate smaller bowl, mix flour, baking soda, baking powder, salt, and chocolate chips.
4. Add dry ingredients to wet ingredients and mix until just combined.
5. Line a 12-cup muffin pan with muffin papers or coat in cooking spray. Fill each muffin cup ⅔ full.
6. Place pans in the oven and bake for 7 minutes at 425°F and then for another 13 minutes at 350°F.
7. Remove from oven when centers are springy.
8. Cool for a few minutes, then remove from pans and serve.

Cinnamon Muffins

Temp: 425°F; 375°F   **Cook Time:** 20 min.

Ingredients:

- ½ cup butter, melted
- ¾ cup milk
- 2 eggs, beaten
- 2 tsp vanilla extract
- 1 ¼ cups sugar
- 2 cups flour
- 1 tsp baking soda
- 3 tsp baking powder
- ½ tsp salt
- 1 tbl ground cinnamon

Topping

- 3 tbls butter, softened
- ½ cup flour
- ¼ cup brown sugar
- ½ tsp ground cinnamon

Instructions:

1. Preheat oven to 425°F.
2. Melt butter in a large mixing bowl and mix in milk, eggs, vanilla, and sugar.
3. In a separate smaller bowl, mix flour, baking soda, baking powder, salt, and cinnamon.
4. Add dry ingredients to wet ingredients and mix until just combined.
5. Line a 12-cup muffin pan with muffin papers or coat in cooking spray. Fill each muffin cup ¾ full.
6. Combine topping ingredients and sprinkle on muffins.
7. Place pans in the oven and bake for 7 minutes at 425°F and then for another 13 minutes at 350°F.
8. Remove from oven when centers are springy.
9. Cool for a few minutes, then remove from pans and serve.

Corn Muffins

Temp: 400°F   **Cook Time:** 15-20 min.

Ingredients:

- 1 ⅓ cups flour
- 1 cup cornmeal
- 6 tbls sugar
- 2 tbls baking powder
- ½ tsp salt
- 14.75 oz creamed corn
- 2 eggs, beaten
- ½ cup milk
- ½ cup sour cream

Instructions:

1. Preheat oven to 400°F.
2. In a medium bowl, whisk together flour, cornmeal, sugar, baking powder, and salt.
3. In a large bowl, mix creamed corn with eggs, milk, and sour cream.
4. Combine all ingredients and pour batter into a greased 12-cup muffin pan.
5. Bake for 15-20 minutes, or until the centers have set.
6. Remove from oven and serve.

Lemon Poppy Seed Muffins

Temp: 375°F   **Cook Time:** 20-40 min.

Ingredients:

- ½ cup butter, melted
- ½ cup milk
- 2 eggs, beaten
- ¼ cup sour cream
- 2 tbls lemon juice
- 1 tsp vanilla extract
- 1 cup sugar
- 2 cups flour

- ½ tsp baking soda
- 2 tsp baking powder
- ½ tsp salt
- 2 tbls poppy seeds

Glaze

- ½ cup powdered sugar
- 1 tbl lemon juice

Instructions:

1. Preheat oven to 375°F.
2. Melt butter in a large mixing bowl and mix in milk, eggs, sour cream, lemon juice, vanilla, and sugar.
3. In a separate smaller bowl, mix flour, baking soda, baking powder, salt, and poppy seeds.
4. Add dry ingredients to the wet ingredients and mix until just combined.
5. Line a 12-cup muffin pan with muffin papers or coat in cooking spray. Fill each muffin cup ⅔ full.
6. Place pans in the oven and bake muffins for 20 minutes or loaves for 35-40 minutes.
7. In a small bowl, combine powdered sugar and lemon juice.
8. Remove from oven when centers are springy, cool for a few minutes, and top with glaze.
9. Remove from pans and serve.

Oatmeal Raisin Muffins

Temp: 425°F; 350°F   **Cook Time:** 20 min.

Ingredients:

- ½ cup butter, melted
- ¾ cup milk
- 2 eggs
- 1 tsp vanilla extract
- 1 cup sugar
- 1 ¼ cups flour
- 1 cup quick oats
- 1 tsp baking soda

- 2 tsp baking powder
- ½ tsp salt
- 1 tsp ground cinnamon
- 1 cup raisins

Glaze

- 2 tbls cream cheese
- ½ cup powdered sugar

Instructions:

1. Preheat oven to 425°F.
2. Melt butter in a large mixing bowl and mix in milk, eggs, vanilla, and sugar.
3. In a separate smaller bowl, mix flour, quick oats, baking soda, baking powder, salt, cinnamon, and raisins.
4. Add dry ingredients to the wet ingredients and mix until just combined.
5. Line a 12-cup muffin pan with muffin papers or coat in cooking spray. Fill each muffin cup ⅔ full.
6. Place pans in the oven and bake for 7 minutes at 425°F and then for another 13 minutes at 350°F.
7. In a small glass bowl, melt the cream cheese and stir in powdered sugar.
8. Remove from oven when centers are springy, cool for a few minutes, and top with cream cheese glaze.
9. Remove from pans and serve.

Pecan Sticky Buns

Temp: 325°F

Cook Time: 35 min.

Ingredients:

- 4 ½ tsp yeast
- ½ cup water, warm
- ½ cup sugar
- .1 ¼ cups buttermilk
- 2 eggs, beaten
- ½ cup butter, softened
- 2 tsp salt
- 5 ½ cups flour
- 2 tsp baking powder

Filling

- ¼ cup butter, softened
- 1 tbl ground cinnamon
- ⅔ cup sugar, or brown sugar

Topping

- ½ cup butter, melted
- ½ cup brown sugar
- 1 cup pecans, chopped

Instructions:

1. Proof yeast in warm water in a large mixing bowl for 10 minutes.
2. Add the remaining ingredients and slowly add the flour, regularly scraping down the sides of the mixing bowl.
3. Knead for 5 minutes. The dough should be soft and sticky.
4. Cover the dough and rise for 1 hour, or until doubled.
5. Divide dough in half and roll each half into a 12x6" rectangle.
6. Cover each piece with half of the butter, sugar, and cinnamon.
7. Roll dough from the short side, pinch the edges, and cut each roll into 12 pieces.
8. Coat two 9" round cake pans with half of the butter, brown sugar, and chopped pecans. Place 12 dough slices in each pan.
9. Rise for 30 minutes. Preheat oven to 325°F.
10. Bake for 35 minutes.
11. Invert pans onto plates upon removing them from the oven.

Cinnamon Bites

Temp: 375°F   **Cook Time:** 20 min.

Ingredients:

- 2 tsp instant yeast
- 3 tbls sugar
- ¾ cup milk, warm
- 4 tbls butter, softened
- 2 cups flour
- ½ tsp baking powder
- ½ tsp salt

Topping
- 4 tbls butter, melted
- 3 tbls sugar
- 1 tsp ground cinnamon

Glaze
- 1 tbl butter, melted
- ½ cup powdered sugar
- 1 tbl milk

Instructions:

1. Dissolve yeast and sugar in warm milk in a large mixing bowl. After 5 minutes, add butter.
2. Mix in flour, baking powder, and salt. The dough will be soft and sticky.
3. Knead on a floured surface to form a soft, elastic dough.
4. Set the dough ball in a bowl, cover, and rise for 30 minutes, or until doubled in size.
5. Scrape dough out onto a floured surface and roll into a 1" log.
6. Cut dough into 1" or smaller pieces and roll pieces into balls.
7. Place in a greased 9x13" baking dish and rise for 15 minutes.
8. Preheat oven to 375°F.
9. Place in oven for 20 minutes, or until golden.
10. Mix the topping in a small bowl and glaze in a separate small bowl.
11. Take dough bites out of the oven, evenly top with cinnamon mixture and glaze, and serve.

Crème Puffs

Temp: 375°F   **Cook Time:** 35 min.

Ingredients:

- ½ cup water
- ½ cup milk
- ½ cup butter
- 1 tsp sugar
- 1 cup flour
- 4-5 eggs

Instructions:

1. Whisk water, milk, butter, and sugar in a saucepan at a low heat, melting everything.
2. Raise temperature to medium-high and bring to a boil.
3. Immediately remove from heat and add flour, stirring until everything is incorporated.
4. Return the pan to the stove at a medium heat for 4 minutes to cook the dough, turning and stirring continuously.
5. Place dough in a medium mixing bowl and stir for 10 minutes to cool dough.
6. Add in beaten eggs one at a time, testing the thickness of the batter. It should fall in a thick ribbon off your spoon. You may find you only need 4 or 4 ½ eggs.
7. Set the dough aside for 30-60 minutes.
8. Preheat oven to 375°F.
9. Using a ¼ cup cookie scoop, place scoops of batter onto a parchment-lined baking sheet.
10. Place one sheet at a time in the oven for 30 minutes.
11. Quickly open the oven door and pierce puffs with a sharp knife. Turn off the oven and bake for another 5 minutes.
12. Remove and serve immediately or fill after they have cooled.

Apple Cider Doughnuts

Temp: 350°F   **Cook Time:** 30 min.

Ingredients:

- 3 cups apple cider
- 3 ½ cups flour
- ⅔ cup brown sugar
- 2 tsp baking powder
- ½ tsp salt
- 1 tsp baking soda
- 1 tsp ground cinnamon
- ½ tsp ground nutmeg

- 1 cup applesauce
- 1 tsp vanilla extract
- 6 tbls butter, melted

Topping

- 6 tbls butter, melted
- 1 cup sugar
- 1 tsp ground cinnamon
- ¼ tsp pie spice

Instructions:

1. Boil apple cider in a small saucepan and reduce to 1 cup. This can take 10-20 minutes. Stir regularly. Cool once reduced.
2. Preheat oven to 350°F.
3. Whisk flour, brown sugar, and remaining dry ingredients in a small bowl.
4. Pour cooled apple cider into a large mixing bowl and mix with applesauce, vanilla, and butter.
5. Add dry ingredients to the wet and stir until just combined.
6. Grease a donut pan and fill with batter to about ⅔ full. This is best done with a piping bag or cut zip-top bag.
7. Place in oven and bake for 9 minutes. If you press the dough and it bounces back, they are done.
   a. Another option is to pipe doughnut shapes onto wax paper, freeze them, and then fry them in 2" of canola oil for 2 minutes on each side at 360°F.
8. Dip doughnuts in melted butter and cover in cinnamon sugar.

Apple Fritters

Temp: 375°F

Cook Time: 20 min.

Ingredients:

- 1 ½ cups flour
- ¼ cup sugar
- 2 tsp baking powder
- ½ tsp salt
- 2 tsp ground cinnamon
- 2 eggs, beaten
- 5 tbls butter, softened
- ⅓ cup milk
- 1 tsp vanilla extract
- 3 cups apples, diced

Cream Cheese Glaze

- 4 oz. cream cheese
- 1 ⅓ cups powdered sugar
- 1 tsp vanilla extract
- 2 tbls milk

- canola oil
- ¼ cup sugar
- 1 tbl ground cinnamon

Instructions:

1. Whisk together dry ingredients in a large bowl.
2. In a second bowl, beat the eggs and add in butter, milk, and vanilla. Then add to the dry ingredients.
3. Fold in the diced apples until just combined.
4. Fill a large pot with 2" of oil and bring to 375°F.
5. Using a ⅓ cup cookie scoop or measuring cup, carefully drop dollops of the batter into the hot oil, careful to keep each one separate so they do not stick together.
6. If needed, spread the dough out to make a wider fritter.
7. Fry each side for 2-3 minutes and then remove and cool on a cooling rack or paper towel.
8. For the glaze, melt the cream cheese in the microwave and quickly stir in the sugar and vanilla. Then stir in the milk.
9. Drizzle glaze and cinnamon sugar on the fritters and serve.

Crullers

Temp: 350°F

Cook Time: 30 min.

Ingredients:

- ½ cup water
- ½ cup milk
- 6 tbls butter
- ½ tbl sugar
- 1 cup flour
- 4 ½ eggs, beaten

- canola oil

Glaze:

- 1 ⅔ cups powdered sugar
- 2 tbls honey
- 4 tbls milk

Instructions:

1. Whisk water, milk, butter, and sugar in a saucepan at a low heat to melt. Raise heat and quickly bring to a boil.
2. Remove from heat and mix in flour with a wooden spatula.
3. Return pan and heat on medium for 4 minutes to cook the dough, turning and stirring continuously.
4. Add dough to a stand mixer or large bowl and stir for 10 minutes to cool.
5. Add in eggs one at a time. The batter should be smooth and glossy. Thick, but should fall off the spatula in ribbons.
6. Cover the dough and set aside for 30 minutes.
7. Heat 2" of oil in a large saucepan to 350°F.
8. Scrape dough into a pastry bag fitted with ½" star tip.
9. Cut out twenty-four 3" square wax paper sheets and pipe a dough circle onto each square.
10. Transfer crullers to oil with the wax paper. Fry for 1 minute on each side, peeling off wax paper between sides.
11. Remove golden crullers from oil and drain on a cookie rack.
12. Mix glaze in a small bowl, dip crullers, and set on the rack.

Glazed Doughnuts

Temp: 350°F

Cook Time: 30 min.

Ingredients:

- 1 cup milk
- ¼ cup butter
- ½ cup sugar
- 3 ½ tsp instant yeast
- ½ cup water, warm
- 1 egg, beaten
- ½ tsp salt

- 4 ½ cups flour
- canola oil

Glaze

- 2 cups powdered sugar
- 2 tbls butter, melted
- 1 tsp vanilla extract
- ¼ cup milk

Instructions:

1. Scald milk in a saucepan until a film forms on the surface. Remove from heat and add butter to the pan.
2. In a large mixing bowl, combine sugar, yeast, and water. Once the milk is at 120°F, add to the mixing bowl.
3. Add the egg and salt to the bowl and combine.
4. Mix in flour one cup at a time and knead in the bowl or on the counter for 5 minutes to form an elastic but sticky dough.
5. Grease a large bowl and set the dough ball inside. Cover the bowl and set it in a warm place for 1 hour or until doubled.
6. Punch down and roll dough on a floured counter to ½" thick.
7. With a donut or biscuit cutter, cut out doughnuts and doughnut holes. Rise for 30 minutes, or until doubled.
8. In a medium bowl, whisk together the glaze ingredients.
9. Add 2" of oil to a large deep pot and heat to 350°F.
10. Use a large metal skimmer to place doughnuts gently into the oil. Fry each side for 1 minute and drain on a paper towel.
11. Dip the doughnuts in the glaze and set on a cooling rack.

Bagels

Temp: 400°F **Cook Time:** 20-25 min.

Ingredients:

- 2 tbls brown sugar
- 2 tsp instant yeast
- 2 tsp salt
- 3 ½ cups bread flour
- ½ cup dried blueberries (optional)
- 1 ¼ cups water, warm

- 6 cups water
- ¼ cup honey

- 1 egg
- 1 tbl water

Instructions:

1. Combine all dry ingredients in a large bowl.
2. Slowly add water and form a soft dough ball.
3. Scrape dough onto a floured surface and knead for 5-10 minutes to form a soft and elastic dough. Shape it into a ball.
4. Spray the mixing bowl with pan spray and set the dough ball inside. Cover for 1 hour to rise until doubled.
5. Preheat oven to 400°F.
6. Place dough on the counter, divide into 8 pieces, and roll into balls. Flour a finger and form a hole in the center, stretching into a ring with a 1 ½" hole. Set aside for 15 minutes.
7. Boil water in a large pot and add honey.
8. Boil bagels for 1 minute per side and remove with a slotted spoon. Drain them on paper towel.
9. Place bagels on two parchment-lined baking sheets.
10. Beat egg with water and brush onto bagels.
11. Bake bagels in the oven for 22-25 minutes until golden brown, rotating sheets halfway through. Cool before serving.

Pretzels

Temp: 425°F

Cook Time: 15-18 min.

Ingredients:

- 1 ½ cups water, warm
- 2 tbls brown sugar
- 3 tsp instant yeast
- 3 tbls butter, melted
- 1 tsp salt
- 4-4 ½ cups flour

- 5 cups water
- ¼ cup baking soda

- 1 egg
- 1 tbl water
- coarse salt

Instructions:

1. Combine water, sugar, yeast, salt, and butter in a large stand mixer mixing bowl.
2. Slowly add flour and knead to form a soft but sticky dough.
3. Scrape dough onto a floured surface and knead for 5 minutes to form a soft and elastic dough. Form into a ball.
4. Spray the mixing bowl with pan spray and set the dough ball inside. Cover for 1 hour to rise until doubled.
5. Preheat oven to 425°F.
6. Boil water in a stock pot and slowly add baking soda.
7. Place dough on the counter, divide into 8-12 pieces, and roll pieces into ropes 20" long and 1" thick. Shape or cut into 1" pretzel bites. Rest the dough for 5 minutes.
8. Boil pretzels for 30 seconds and remove with a slotted spoon.
9. Drain the dough and place on a parchment-lined baking pan.
10. Mix egg with water and brush pretzels, topping with salt.
11. Bake pretzels in oven for 15-18 minutes until golden brown.
12. Remove from oven and serve.
13. If desired, brush with butter and dust with cinnamon sugar.

Pies, Crisps, and Cakes

Pie Crust

Temp: 375°F   **Cook Time:** 25 min.

Ingredients:

- 2 ½ cups pastry or all-purpose flour
- 1 tsp salt
- 1 tbl sugar
- 1 cup butter, cold
- 2 egg yolks
- 3-4 tbls ice water

Instructions:

1. Mix flour, salt, and sugar in a food processor or mixing bowl.
2. Add in the cold butter chopped in pieces and process for about twenty seconds or blend with a pastry blender until it resembles coarse crumbs.
3. Add in two egg yolks and beat with cold water.
4. Using a food processor or your hands, form dough into a ball. If using a processor, do not over mix or it will become tough.
   a. The dough can be refrigerated for up to three days or frozen when tightly wrapped in plastic wrap.
5. If using now, roll out and lay pie crusts into two 10" pie pans and prick the bottom. Cover with plastic wrap and set in the refrigerator for 20 minutes.
6. Preheat oven to 375°F.
7. Lay down a sheet of parchment paper onto the crust and add a layer of dried beans. Bake for 25 minutes.
8. Remove parchment and pie weights and add pie filling of choice.

Any Name Would Be as Sweet

"What is that one called?"

Eddie sighed and looked up from the dirt he was packing around a tomato plant. His knees ached, and his back was exhausted from his posture on the ground. Yet this was his sanctum, and the question pulled him from his reverie.

"It's a Gerber daisy."

"And what is this one?"

"Probably a petunia."

She hopped a few feet away, touching the flowers as she passed. Hmph. At least she was quiet again. There were no petunias in this garden, and he had not bought any Gerber daisies yet, but they were the first to come to mind and they appeased her curious mind. He turned back to his tomato plant, finished packing in the dirt, and moved on to the next one. Eddie dug a small hole with his trowel, carefully tugged out the roots from its plastic cage, and set the plant in the hole. He packed some more dirt an-

"How about this one?"

Startled, he looked up. She was pointing to another flower in a different section of the garden nearly fifteen feet away. How was he supposed to see that?

"'How about this one' what?"

"How about its name?"

Turning back to his tomato plant, "It's an aster."

He heard her repeat the name and then skip over to the other side of the yard. Tapping a bit of dirt around the last plant, he gathered his tools and brought them around the side of the house. Where did that sapling go? He wanted to get it planted today before it wilted like half of the annuals that littered the driveway. There it is, behind the tabl-

"What is this one?"

In her hand, Joey held a flower with yellow petals and a black center. She must have gone digging for those.

"It's a black-eyed Susan."

She scrunched up her nose. "That's a funny name. Are you sure? It looks like a sunflower."

"Positive." Eddie picked up a shovel and the sapling and made his way toward the middle of the yard. Joey's steps hastened to follow him. Staying far enough back to keep dirt off her shoes, she watched as he broke apart the ground and dug a deep hole. Hopefully, this would only take a few min-

"Why is this one so deep?"

"So deep? Compared to what?" Eddie stuck the shovel in the ground and lit a cigarette.

"The holes for the tomato plants weren't nearly as deep. This one will go to China."

He coughed. "No, it won't go that far, but trees need deep roots, for water."

"Oh." He watched as she pondered this for a moment, then finished his digging. Back on his knees again, he set the sapling into the hole. Joey came down and brushed dirt over the tiny roots.

"What is this?" she inquired once more.

"The label," he voiced around his cigarette.

"A peach tree," she read. "Will we have peaches this year?"

"No." He stood back up, dusted his knees, and put his tools away by the side of the house. Joey was still sitting by the peach tree. Moving inside to wash his hands, he tuned out the prattle of Ida. She only said the same things anyway. Out the kitchen window, he could see Joey watering the peach tree. He had forgotten. Hard not to with all the chatter. Hopefully, she didn't drown it.

Eddie dried his hands, and in a moment, heard the crash of the back door as Joey bounded inside.

"Mom! Dad and I planted the garden today!"

Ida continued half listening as Joey expounded on their task. But Eddie smiled. After all, they had.

Apple Pie

Temp: 375°F, 425°F   **Cook Time:** 1 hr.

Ingredients:

- 5 cups apples, sliced
- ½ cup sugar
- ¼ cup brown sugar
- 1 tsp ground cinnamon
- ¼ tsp ground nutmeg
- ⅛ tsp ground cloves
- ⅛ tsp salt
- 2 tbls flour
- 1 batch of pie crust (p. 219)
- 3 tbls butter, melted

Instructions:

1. Preheat the oven to 375°F.
2. Make the pie crust (p. 219). Roll out half and set it in a 10" pie dish. Wrap the crust and the other half in plastic wrap and set in the refrigerator for 20 minutes.
3. Add pie weights and bake the crust for 20 minutes at 375°F.
4. While the crust bakes, slice the apples and toss them with the sugars, spices, and flour.
5. Remove the crust from the oven and set the temperature to 425°F.
6. Pour apples onto the baked crust and roll out the other half.
7. Lay the top crust onto the apples and crimp the edges. Slice five slits into the top of the pie.
8. Place in oven and bake for 25 minutes.
9. Brush all the melted butter onto the crust and bake for another 10 minutes.
10. Remove from oven, cool, and serve.

Blueberry Pie

Temp: 375°F **Cook Time:** 45-60 min.

Ingredients:

- 1 batch of pie crust (p. 219)
- blueberry filling (p. 168).
- 2 tbls butter, melted
- 2 tbls sugar

Instructions:

1. Make blueberry filling (p. 168). Set in refrigerator to cool completely.
2. Make pie crust (p. 219). Form half of the crust into a 10" pie dish and cover it in plastic wrap. Wrap the other half and set both in the refrigerator for 20 minutes.
3. Preheat oven to 375°F.
4. Remove the filling and crust from the refrigerator. Pour filling into preformed pie crust.
5. Roll out the other half of the dough and slice into 10" long strips ½" wide. You will need at least 10 strips.
6. Weave these strips on top of the dough and crimp the edge of the pie.
7. Place in oven and bake for 30 minutes.
8. Brush with butter and dust with sugar.
9. Bake for another 15-30 minutes, or until the crust is golden and the filling is bubbling.
10. Remove pie from oven, cool if desired, and serve.

Lemon Meringue Pie

Temp: 350°F

Cook Time: 10 min.

Ingredients:

Lemon Filling

- 1 ¼ cups sugar
- 6 tbls cornstarch
- ⅔ cup lemon juice
- 4 egg yolks
- 1 ½ cups boiling water
- 2 tbls butter

- 10" baked pie crust (p. 219)

Meringue

- 4 egg whites
- 6 tbls sugar

Instructions:

7. Begin making the lemon filling.
8. In a medium saucepan, whisk together sugar, cornstarch, and lemon juice.
9. Beat egg yolks in a small bowl. Add to lemon mixture.
10. Turn heat to medium and, while constantly stirring, gradually add in water.
11. Stir for 6-8 minutes until the mixture boils and thickens.
12. Remove from heat and stir in butter.
13. Pour lemon into baked 10" crust.
14. Preheat oven to 350°F.
15. For the meringue, beat egg whites until soft peaks form.
16. Slowly add sugar, beating until stiff peaks form.
17. Use a spatula to spread meringue over the lemon filling. It does not need to be smooth.
18. Place in oven for 20 minutes until meringue turns golden.
19. Remove from oven and cool on the counter for 1 hour.
20. Refrigerate for at least 2 hours before serving.

Lemon Supreme Pie

Ingredients:

- 10" baked pie crust (p. 219)
- 16 oz. whipped cream

Cheesecake filling

- 3.4 oz. cheesecake pudding mix
- ½ cup milk
- 8 oz. cream cheese, soft

- 1 cup whipped cream

Lemon Filling

- 1 ¼ cups sugar
- 6 tbls cornstarch
- ⅔ cup lemon juice
- 4 egg yolks
- 1 ½ cups water, boiling
- 2 tbls butter

Instructions:

1. Begin making the cheesecake filling by first mixing pudding mix and milk, then cream cheese, and then whipped cream.
2. Spread on the bottom of the baked 10" pie crust and set in the refrigerator while making the lemon filling.
3. In a medium saucepan, whisk together sugar, cornstarch, and lemon juice.
4. Beat egg yolks in a small bowl. Add to lemon mixture.
5. Turn heat to medium and, while constantly stirring, gradually add in water.
6. Stir for 6-8 minutes until the mixture boils and thickens.
7. Remove from heat and stir in butter.
8. Pour lemon over the cheesecake. Depending on how deep your pie dish is, there may be some left over. Refrigerate for an hour.
9. Top with whipped cream using either a spatula or a pastry bag with a large star tip and serve.

Pumpkin Pie

Temp: 425°F, 325°F   **Cook Time:** 1 hr.

Ingredients:

- 29 oz. pure pumpkin
- 1 tsp vanilla extract
- 4 eggs, beaten
- 2 cups evaporated milk
- 1 ½ cups brown sugar
- 1 tsp salt
- 2 tbls flour
- 1 tsp ground cinnamon
- ½ tsp ground ginger
- ¼ tsp ground cloves
- ½ tsp ground nutmeg
- 2 unbaked pie crusts (p. 219)

Instructions:

1. Preheat oven to 425°F.
2. Stir together pumpkin, vanilla, eggs, and milk until just combined.
3. Whisk together dry ingredients in a small bowl and then stir into pumpkin.
4. Pour into two unbaked 10" pie crusts.
5. Place pies in oven and bake at 425°F for 15 minutes.
6. Turn down the temperature to 325°F and bake for another 45 minutes until the filling is firm. You should be able to stick a knife in the middle and have it come out clean.
7. Remove from oven, cool, and serve.

Pecan Pie

Temp: 350°F   **Cook Time:** 45-60 min.

Ingredients:

- 10" unbaked pie crust (p. 219)
- ⅓ cup butter
- ½ cup honey or dark corn syrup
- ½ cup brown sugar
- ⅓ cup dark brown sugar
- 1 tsp vanilla extract
- ½ tsp salt
- 2 eggs, beaten
- 2 cups pecans, chopped

Instructions:

1. Preheat oven to 350°F.
2. Melt and combine butter, brown sugar, vanilla, and salt in a medium saucepan.
3. As soon as it begins to simmer, remove from heat.
4. Bcat eggs in a large bowl until they are frothy.
5. Stir pecans into eggs.
6. Slowly whisk the sugar mixture into the eggs.
7. Pour into a 10" pie crust.
8. Place in oven and bake for 45-60 minutes, or until the filling has set.
9. Remove from oven and cool.
10. Once cooled, cut and serve.

Fruit Crisp

Temp: 375°F

Cook Time: 30 min.

Ingredients:

- 5 cups fruit
- 2 tbls sugar
- 2 tbls brown sugar
- 2 tsp ground cinnamon
- 2 tbls flour

Streusel Topping

- 1 ¼ cups flour
- ¾ cup brown sugar
- ¼ cup sugar
- 1 tsp ground cinnamon
- ½ cup butter, softened

Crumble Topping

- ½ cup rolled oats
- ½ cup flour
- ¾ cup brown sugar
- ¼ cup chopped nuts
- ½ tsp ground cinnamon
- ½ tsp ground nutmeg
- ½ cup butter, cold

Instructions:

1. Preheat oven to 375°F.
2. Toss fruit in a large bowl with sugars, cinnamon, and flour.
3. Pour into a 9x9" baking dish or a large pie dish.
4. In that bowl, mix the dry topping ingredients for either the streusel or crumble topping and then cut in butter.
5. Coat the fruit evenly with the crumble or streusel topping evenly.
6. Place in oven and bake for 30 minutes until the top is golden.
7. Remove from oven and serve with ice cream.

Peach Cobbler

Temp: 425°F   **Cook Time:** 40 min.

Ingredients:

- 12 peaches
- ¼ cup white sugar
- ¼ cup brown sugar
- ½ tsp ground cinnamon
- ¼ tsp ground nutmeg
- 2 tsp cornstarch

Dusting

- 3 tbls white sugar
- 1 tsp ground cinnamon

Cobbler Topping

- 6 tbls butter, cold
- 1 cup flour
- ¼ cup white sugar
- ¼ cup brown sugar
- 1 tsp baking powder
- ½ tsp salt
- ¼ cup boiling water

Instructions:

1. Pit peaches and slice them into 1/16ths. Place in a large bowl.
2. Preheat oven to 425°F.
3. Add sugars, spices, and cornstarch to the peaches and toss until the peaches are evenly coated.
4. Pour peaches into a 9x13" baking dish and bake for 10 minutes.
5. While the peaches bake, combine flour, sugars, baking powder, and salt.
6. Cut butter into flour mixture with a pastry blender.
7. Stir in water until just combined.
8. Remove peaches from the oven and top with the cobbler mixture.
9. Return to oven and bake for an additional 30 minutes until the cobbler topping is golden.
10. Remove from oven and dust with cinnamon sugar mixture.

"Grandma's Cake" from *The American*

It was good to be back in Pennsylvania, and the fact that they could be here for a whole month was perfect. Despite her initial run, Ida now sat beside him, happily married. Well, happily could be an overstatement, but perhaps her shouting was the voice of affection. He would never complain. The lawn out back was smaller now, smaller than he remembered. A chicken coop ran along the back fence of the yard and the garden had grown in width. His mother had shown it to him earlier, and they spent time talking and tending while Ida made a cake for dessert.

Helen came out on the porch and said, "Ed, Ida, dinner is done, and you need to come in now. These Gołąbki will not eat themselves!"

He stood and held out a hand to help up his wife, smiling at her and then at the yard. Together they walked into the house to eat with his family. His father was tired, but he could still see the twinkling of pride in his eyes every time they looked at each other. After praying, they ate and talked. Helen wanted to know if they were staying in Michigan. They were. His mother asked if she and Papa would be Dziadek and Babcia. Ida said hopefully soon. They had a little house in Detroit now; all that was left was to fill it.

Ida left the table and came back with the cake she had made earlier. She cut a slice for each of them and served it beautifully, her husband smiling at her with pride. Then each of them took a bite and grimaced at the awful flavor in their mouths. Ida, having not noticed the looks on everyone's faces, did the same and was the first to make a sound.

"Augh, what is this? What happened"

Everyone looked at each other, unsure of what to say that would not upset her more. But Helen spoke, "The cake tastes rather salty."

They went to the kitchen and found that the bags of salt and sugar were remarkably similar, concluding that the ingredients must have been switched in the process of making the cake.

"No worries, dear," Helen said to her muttering sister-in-law, "We will just feed the cake to the chickens."

Together, they went out to toss the cake in the yard for the already fat birds. While they were out, Benjamin whispered to his son that maybe he should stick to the cooking from now on. Edward told his father that this was a rare, one-time-only treat, and they laughed. Thankfully, the night was not ruined. Feliksa had sent her daughter to the market for some kołaczki earlier that day before she had known about the cake. Before long, the disaster was forgotten and they were able to finish out their night in peace.

Morning came and Edward made them breakfast. Polish pancakes were in order. Soon, the smell of fried bacon filled the house and woke its inhabitants. His mother's jam wrapped in the eggy dough was the perfect start to the morning. Ida came down next and soon all of them sat about the table to eat breakfast. They sat silently. Edward, looking 'round and enjoying the satisfied faces of his family, was content with this these moments until he saw the startled look covering his mother's face. He turned to look out the window where her gaze went and saw the same scene. They both walked outside and found the fluffy bodies of the birds lying behind their fence. Not a feather was out of place, and not a crumb of cake remained.

Apple Coffee Cake

Temp: 350°F

Cook Time: 45 min.

Ingredients:

- ½ cup butter, softened
- 1 ½ cups brown sugar
- 2 eggs, beaten
- 2 tsp vanilla extract
- 1 cup sour cream
- 2 cups flour
- 1 tsp baking soda
- 1 tsp ground cinnamon
- 1 tsp pie spice
- ½ tsp salt
- 2 cups apples, chopped

Topping

- ½ cup brown sugar
- ½ cup flour
- ¼ tsp ground cinnamon
- ¼ tsp pie spice
- 4 tbls butter, softened

Glaze

- ½ cup brown sugar
- ½ tsp vanilla extract
- 2 tbls butter, melted
- 1 tbl milk

Instructions:

1. Preheat oven to 350°F.
2. Cream butter and brown sugar in a medium bowl.
3. Beat in eggs and add vanilla and sour cream.
4. Mix dry ingredients in a small bowl and stir into wet ingredients.
5. Mix in apples and pour into a greased 9x13" baking dish.
6. In the small bowl, combine the dry topping ingredients and cut in butter. Sprinkle over batter.
7. Bake for 45 minutes, or until the center is springy.
8. Mix glaze ingredients in a small bowl.
9. Remove pan from oven, cool, and drizzle glaze over the cake before serving.

Banana Cake

Temp: 350°F   **Cook Time:** 40-50 min.

Ingredients:

- 3 cups flour
- 1 ½ cups sugar
- 1 tsp baking powder
- 1 tsp baking soda
- ½ tsp salt
- 1 ½ cups ripe bananas, mashed (3-4 bananas)
- 1 ½ cups buttermilk
- ¾ cup butter, softened
- 2 tsp vanilla extract
- 3 eggs, beaten
- ¾ cup walnuts, chopped (optional)

Instructions:

1. Preheat oven to 350°F.
2. Whisk together flour, sugar, baking powder, baking soda, and salt in a medium bowl.
3. Mash bananas in a large bowl and beat in buttermilk, butter, vanilla, and eggs.
4. Slowly mix dry ingredients into the wet ingredients. Add walnuts, if desired.
5. Pour batter into a greased 9x13" pan and bake for 40-50 minutes, or into three greased 8" or 9" round cake pans and bake for 25-30 minutes.
6. Remove from oven when the middle of the cake bounces back when pressed.
7. Cool for 20 minutes then remove from pans and frost.

Carrot Cake

Temp: 325°F

Cook Time: 50-60 min.

Ingredients:

- 2 cups flour
- 1 ½ cups sugar
- ½ cup brown sugar
- 1 tsp baking powder
- 1 tsp baking soda
- 1 tsp salt
- 1 ½ tsp ground cinnamon
- 3 cups carrots, shredded

- 1 cup vegetable oil
- 4 eggs, beaten

Frosting

- 8 oz. cream cheese
- 2 tsp vanilla extract
- ½ cup butter, softened
- 4 cups powdered sugar

Instructions:

1. Preheat oven to 325°F.
2. Whisk together flour, sugars, baking powder, baking soda, salt, and cinnamon in a medium bowl.
3. In a large bowl, mix carrots, oil, and eggs.
4. Slowly add dry ingredients to wet ingredients.
5. Pour batter into two greased 8" cake pans.
6. Bake for 50-60 minutes, or until the middle of the cake bounces back when pressed.
7. Remove from oven, cool, and remove from pans.
8. Slice off any rounded tops with a knife or metal spatula.
9. In a small bowl, whip frosting ingredients.
10. Using a metal spatula or butter knife, spread frosting on one layer of cake, set the second layer on top, and cover the rest of the cake with frosting and serve.

Earthquake Cake

Temp: 350°F   **Cook Time:** 35 min.

Ingredients:

- 1 cup unsweetened shredded coconut
- 1 cup pecans, chopped
- 15.25 oz. German chocolate cake mix
- 2 oz. instant chocolate pudding mix
- 4 eggs, beaten
- ½ cup butter, melted
- 1 ⅓ cups half and half
- ½ cup chocolate chips
- 6 oz. cream cheese, softened
- ¼ cup butter, melted
- 1 tsp vanilla extract
- 2 cups powdered sugar

Instructions:

1. Preheat oven to 350°F.
2. In a greased 9x13" baking dish, layer coconut and pecans.
3. In a large bowl, combine cake mix with the pudding mix, eggs, butter, and half and half.
4. Pour batter over pecans and coconut.
5. Sprinkle chocolate chips over the batter.
6. In a small bowl, blend cream cheese, butter, vanilla, and powdered sugar.
7. Pour cream cheese over the batter and swirl with a spatula.
8. Bake for 35 minutes. The middle will still be soft but should not jiggle when finished.
9. Remove from oven and serve.

Texas Sheet Cake

Temp: 350°F

Cook Time: 15-20 min.

Ingredients:

- 2 cups flour
- 2 cups sugar
- 1 tsp baking soda
- ½ tsp salt
- ½ cup sour cream
- 2 eggs, beaten
- 1 cup butter, melted
- ⅓ cup cocoa powder
- 1 cup water
- 1 tsp vanilla extract

Icing

- ⅓ cup milk
- ½ cup butter, melted
- ⅓ cup cocoa powder
- 3 cups powdered sugar
- 2 tsp vanilla extract

Instructions:

1. Preheat oven to 350°F.
2. Whisk flour, sugar, baking soda, and salt in a large bowl.
3. Beat sour cream and eggs in a small bowl and mix into the dry ingredients.
4. Melt butter in a small saucepan and whisk in cocoa and water.
5. Remove from heat, add vanilla, and stir into the rest of the batter.
6. Pour batter into a greased 9x13" or 11x15" baking dish.
7. Bake for 15-20 minutes, or until the cake has set.
8. Whisk butter and milk in the saucepan and bring to a boil.
9. Remove from heat and stir in cocoa, powdered sugar, and vanilla.
10. Remove the cake from the oven and pour icing over the cake.
11. Once the icing has set, cut, and serve.

My Life as a Child Cake Tester

It was a beautiful thing to behold. It was also the biggest mess. And it was glorious. Imagine, if you will, a Jackson Pollack painting. Blacks, blues, purples, a hint of green and red, and a dash of orange, mixed with white. Now take that, put it in frosting form, and smear it all over a toddler. That was the masterpiece that sat before us on the canvas of my youngest brother's exuberant face. My mom was a mixture of horror and laughter. My brother and I were all giggles. The three of us were a sight to behold, but not even we could compare to the modern art spectacle taking place on my youngest brother's face, hands, chest, and walker tray.

Mixers are very loud, you see. On a normal day at a normal speed, you can probably talk over their noise. But when you have three running at full speed, beating buttercream frosting to peak perfection, you cannot hear a thing, least of all a small child's squeaky walker moving from one side of the basement to the side of the counter where there is a garbage can with discarded frosting at just the right height for the aforementioned small child. What a mess. But what a memory.

This is probably one of my favorite memories of my mom making cakes, though there are some other great ones. Like watching my mom make the green and teal sponge-painted cake with white and yellow flowers. I barely needed to voice my concern before my mom answered the look on my face. It was hideous, yet my mom made it beautiful. There was also the brown and orange art deco cake that was "just perfect" for the recipient. And I could never forget the candy cake. Oh my. Each layer was covered with hand-set candies of every sort: gummy bears, Pez, M&M's, Nerds, and I think some Twizzlers. Then at the top, the crème de la crème: Barbie and Mr. Potato Head (in a leather biker jacket). My mom was really unsure about that one, but she'd rarely seen a happier bride upon viewing their cake for the first time. Hey, the bride is always right, right?

There were perks to being a kid whose mom made cakes professionally in the home, too. And I do not just mean garbage can frosting (that was a treat only my littlest brother could devise). No, the best parts were cake crunchies. What are cake crunchies, you ask? Well, in order to get a perfectly smooth cake, you need to slice off the top and sometimes the sides. This results in a LOT of leftover cake. White cake, chocolate cake, yellow cake, marble cake, red velvet cake — you name it, we had it. And we got to eat it warm.

After my mom would finish making the edges smooth, she would call up the stairs, "Cake crunchies!" And like the herd of elephants we were, my brother and I would race down, grab what we could, and run back up. Sometimes, while the mixers were on, we would sneak down again and grab some more. It was just asking us, after all. They were just sitting there, those mounds of leftover cake, teetering on the edge of the counter only moments from falling into the trash and a pile of leftover frosting. It would be a travesty to just throw it all away. And hey, that was way too much cake for one small, increasingly mobile child who was just as likely to steal it from the trash. My brother and I were heroes, really. And this was a sacrifice we as personal cake testers were willing to make.

Box Cake Mix

Temp: 350°F   **Cook Time:** 18-28 min.

Ingredients:

One Box:

- 15.25 oz. cake mix
- 4 eggs
- ½ cup vegetable oil
- 1 ⅓ cups half and half
- 2 oz. instant pudding mix

Three Boxes:

- 3 boxes yellow or chocolate cake mix
- 10 eggs
- 1 ½ cups vegetable oil
- 4 cups half and half
- 5.9 oz. instant pudding mix

Instructions:

1. Preheat oven to 350°F.
2. Add all ingredients to a large stand mixer and blend smooth.
3. Fill greased pans with batter:
    a. 1 box: three 6" round pans or one 8x12" baking sheet or 24 cupcakes.
    b. 2 boxes: three 10" round pans or one 13x18" baking sheet + 6 cupcakes or a 5" round pan.
    c. 3 boxes (4 white box mix): two 13x18" baking sheets.
4. Place round or sheet pans in the oven for 24-28 minutes and cupcakes for 18-21 minutes.
5. Remove when centers are springy and cool completely.
6. Remove from pans and cut off tops and sides if necessary to have a straight edge for frosting and leftover cake crunchies.
7. A round or square cake should have three layers of cake with two frosting or filling layers. Sheet or half-sheet cakes should be two layers of cake with one layer of frosting or filling.

Cherry Chip Cake

Temp: 350°F   **Cook Time:** 18-28 min.

Ingredients:

- 15.25 oz. white or yellow cake mix
- 4 eggs (3 for white cake)
- ½ cup vegetable oil
- ¾ cup half and half
- ⅔ cup maraschino cherry juice
- ½ cup maraschino cherries, minced
- 3.9 oz. instant vanilla pudding mix

Instructions:

1. Preheat oven to 350°F.
2. Add all ingredients to a large stand mixer and blend smooth.
3. Fill greased pans with batter:
   a. 1 box: three 6" round pans or one 8x12" baking sheet or 24 cupcakes.
   b. 2 boxes: three 10" round pans or one 13x18" baking sheet + 6 cupcakes or a 5" round pan.
   c. 3 boxes (4 white box mix): two 13x18" baking sheets.
4. Place round pans or sheet pans in the oven for 24-28 minutes and cupcakes for 18-21 minutes.
5. Remove when centers are springy and cool completely.
6. Remove from pans and cut off tops and sides if necessary to have a straight edge for frosting and leftover cake crunchies.
7. A round or square cake should have three layers of cake with two frosting or filling layers. Sheet or half sheet cakes should be two layers of cake with one layer of frosting or filling.

Cake Pops

Ingredients:

- 15.25 oz. cake mix (p. 240)
- 2 cups frosting
- 20 sucker sticks
- 24 oz. chocolate bark or chips, melted

Instructions:

1. Bake cake according to package instructions and cool.
2. Crumble cake in a mixing bowl and combine with frosting.
3. Form eighteen to twenty 1" balls with a cookie scoop and set on a parchment-lined baking sheet.
4. Melt the chocolate in a small bowl.
5. Dip one end of the sucker stick into the chocolate and insert it into the cake ball.
6. Refrigerate for 30 minutes.
7. Dip cake pops into melted chocolate and either place upside down onto the baking sheet for the chocolate to set or stick into a styrofoam base to create a rounder shape.
8. Drizzle with chocolate and sprinkle with cookie crumbs, chopped nuts, or sprinkles. Serve once the chocolate has set.
   a. Options: Red velvet cake + cream cheese frosting dipped in white chocolate. Yellow cake + 1 cup frosting + ½ cup raspberry or strawberry jam dipped in dark chocolate. Chocolate cake + ¾ cup chocolate frosting + 1 cup coconut pecan frosting dipped in milk chocolate. Chocolate cake + ¾ cup buttercream + ¾ cup minced cherry pie filling dipped in milk chocolate.

Pride Cometh Before a Fall

As I have mentioned, there were many perks to being a child of a cake decorator. There were also some downsides. One of those was having to spend almost every weekend in the summer driving around in a freezing car while my mom delivered cakes to various halls, churches, and high schools. I suppose it was not all bad. I mean, don't get me wrong, the cold was something I hated. But my brother and I even got to get out sometimes and help by holding open doors. Then we would take the chance to explore a little bit, so long as we did not touch anything. Getting to see all of the pretty halls set up for a wedding was fun.

Even now, I can still remember some of the cakes we delivered. When I see pictures from my mom's example album, I can recognize some of them. Sometimes I would come downstairs while she was decorating and sit quietly while she worked on and decorated the cake. I would watch as she would mix colors and roll out fondant. Sometimes I would help make flowers or brush on pearl dust. She would measure and cut dowl rods for stacking cakes (I still marvel at how many cakes she could stack). She did not always put the whole thing together before delivering it, at least not that I can remember, but it was fun to see them in their partial glory.

There were also some weird ones. My mom always made wonderful, delicious cakes, and always what the bride (or her mother) ordered. But sometimes I do not think some people actually thought through what they ordered. But every time, the bride would gush over how much she just loved her cakes. There is no accounting for taste, I suppose.

Speaking of brides coming in and gushing over their cakes, my mom did not like to be watched while she was setting up (or having anyone help besides her asking). Like a painter mid-masterpiece, you would not come up and say, "Are you sure that's supposed to look like that?" As if they were there when she put the eggs in the batter! I am sure it didn't look much like a masterpiece when Michelangelo mixed colors on a palette either. Still, people would come up and ask questions or make comments, and each time my mom would say, "I'm not finished yet." And each time we would all be amazed.

Once, she did ask someone for help. Well, twice in one day. But we will get to that. I honestly cannot remember if I went on this trip, but I am pretty sure my brother did. Maybe I was home with my youngest brother? Anyway, cake tables are not always in the same place, you see. Sometimes they are the room's centerpiece, sometimes they are off to the side. It all depends on the hall and the bride. My mom, being the artist, did not always like how a particular table was set or the angle her cake was at. So once, she asked one of the workers at the hall if he could help her move a table.

"Sure," he said, "Are you sure it won't fall over?"

My mom laughed. "My cakes never fall," she said.

He looked unconvinced, but he came over to help. The cake was centered on the foundation of a flimsy folding table, and together my mom and the worker picked up and moved it so that it was just to her liking.

"See? I told you. They never fall."

He nodded, no longer needing to be convinced, and went back to his work. My mom finished her work, adding whatever tiny details she saw fit, and went back home to pick up her next cake.

She went to the next hall, unloaded everything, and started setting up the cake. As I said before, cake tables are different in every hall. This was a multi-tiered cake on top of a fountain in the middle of a round table. Now, these tables are very wide, and my mom is very short. So, she would put the cake together off-centered and then push the cake towards the middle. She had done this dozens of times. It was old hat. Except for today.

Before she could stop it, the cake on top of the fountain fell over and onto the table, and at that moment, the mother of the bride walked in. My mom burst into tears. Thankfully, my mom knew the mother of the bride. Even more thankfully, she had brought extra supplies to fix said cake. To be fair, it was not entirely salvageable, but she was able to make the centerpiece cake look gorgeous. So gorgeous, in fact, that the bride never noticed. After all, my mom is an artist, and a miracle worker at that. But one thing she never said after that was, "My cakes never ___." Because pride truly does cometh before a fall.

The Frosting Recipe

Ingredients:

- 1 ½ lbs. Sweetex (high ratio shortening)
- 1 lb. white margarine (oleo)
- ½ lb. butter
- 2 tsp vanilla extract
- 6-7 cups powdered sugar (2 lbs. = 7 ½ cups)

Instructions:

1. Take out Sweetex, margarine, and butter and set on the counter for 15-20 minutes. They should be just cooler than room temperature when you begin. Too warm, and the frosting will not be fluffy, so do not leave out longer than 30 minutes.
2. Add Sweetex, margarine, and butter to a 5 qt. stand mixer.
3. Whip the fats until they are more than doubled in volume.
4. Once the fats have been well-whipped, add vanilla and 6 cups powdered sugar to the bowl, whipping continually and scraping down the bowl regularly.
5. If you like a sweeter frosting, add 7-7 ½ cups powdered sugar.
6. When you are finished, you will have 5 qts. of frosting.

Coconut Pecan Frosting

Ingredients:

- 1 cup sugar
- 1 cup brown sugar
- 1 cup butter
- 1 ½ cups evaporated milk
- 3 eggs, beaten
- 1 tsp vanilla extract
- 2 ½ cups sweetened shredded coconut
- 2 cups pecans, chopped and toasted

Instructions:

1. Add sugar, butter, milk, vanilla, and eggs to a 3-quart saucepan.
2. Whisk constantly over a medium heat for 6-8 minutes until the mixture has thickened and is bubbling.
3. Remove from heat and stir in coconut and pecans.
4. Cool for 30 minutes, stirring occasionally.
5. Once cool and spreadable, use it to frost cake.

Chocolate Mousse

Ingredients:

- ½ batch of The Frosting Recipe (p. 246)
- 5.9 oz. instant chocolate pudding mix
- 3 cups milk, cold

Instructions:

1. Prepare a half batch of frosting.
2. Whip pudding mix into the milk in a large mixing bowl.
3. Refrigerate for 30 minutes.
4. Whip pudding into frosting and refrigerate for 30 minutes before using in a cake.

Cream Cheese Frosting

Ingredients:

- 8 oz. cream cheese
- ½ cup butter
- 3 cups powdered sugar
- 1 tsp vanilla extract

Instructions:

1. Set cream cheese and butter on the counter about 15-20 minutes before you begin so that they are slightly colder than room temperature.
2. Whip cream cheese and butter in a large mixing bowl until fluffy.
3. Add vanilla and powdered sugar 1 cup at a time.
4. This will make enough frosting for the top of a 9x13 cake. For the sides of a sheet cake or an 8-9" round cake, double the recipe.

Fruit Cream Filling

Ingredients:

- ½ batch of The Frosting Recipe (p. 246)
- 2 cups fruit preserves, lemon curd, or pie filling

Instructions:

1. Prepare a half batch of frosting.
2. Whip in the fruit preserves, lemon curd, or pie filling. If the filling or preserves have large chunks of fruit (such as cherry or blueberry), puree in a food processor first.
3. Keep cold and covered until ready to use in a cake.

Cookies, Bars, and Treats

Bachelor Cookies

Cook Time: 10 min.

Ingredients:

- ½ cup butter
- ½ cup milk
- 2 cups sugar
- ½ cup cocoa powder
- 1 tsp vanilla extract
- ¼ cup peanut butter (or butter)
- 3 cups quick oats

Instructions:

1. Melt butter, milk, sugar, and cocoa powder in a medium saucepan and bring to a simmer.
2. Whisk for about 3 minutes until the mixture is smooth.
3. Add vanilla and peanut butter, or extra butter, to the mixture, stir, and turn off the heat.
4. Add oats to the mixture and combine quickly.
5. Using a 2 tbls cookie scoop, scoop out cookies onto two parchment-covered baking sheets.
6. Refrigerate for 1 hour before serving.

Cappuccino Butter Cookies

Temp: 400°F   **Cook Time:** 6-10 min.

Ingredients:

- ¼ cup water, hot
- 1 tbl instant coffee granules
- 1 cup butter, softened
- 1 cup sugar
- 1 egg, beaten
- 1 tsp baking powder
- 2 ½ cups flour

Instructions:

1. Dissolve coffee in hot water.
2. Combine butter, sugar, and egg.
3. Add coffee to wet ingredients.
4. Add flour and baking powder and form a soft dough.
5. Roll dough into a 2" thick log, wrap in plastic wrap, and chill for 1 hour. Once chilled, slice into ½" thick disks.
   a. Alternatively, cover the dough and chill for 1 hour. Roll out dough on a floured surface and cut with cookie cutters.
6. Place cookies onto a parchment covered baking sheet.
7. Bake at 400°F for 6 to 10 minutes.
8. Remove from oven, cool, and serve.
9. If desired, freeze cookies after baking for 30 minutes. Dip cold cookies halfway into melted chocolate and place on a parchment-lined baking sheet for the chocolate to set.

Chocolate Chip Cookies

Temp: 350°F   **Cook Time:** 8-10 min.

Ingredients:

- 8 tbls butter, melted
- ¼ cup sugar
- ½ cup brown sugar
- 1 tsp vanilla extract
- 1 egg, beaten
- 1 ½ cups flour
- ½ tsp baking soda
- ¼ tsp salt
- 1 cup chocolate chips

Instructions:

1. Preheat oven to 350°F.
2. Combine butter with sugars, vanilla, and egg.
3. Mix in dry ingredients, then mix in chocolate chips.
4. Scoop out eighteen cookies with a 1 ½ tbls cookie scoop onto a parchment-covered baking sheet.
5. Bake for 8-10 minutes. The edges will be golden but the centers soft when they leave the oven.
6. Let them sit for a few minutes on the baking sheet and serve.
   a. Alternatively, reduce flour to 1 ¼ cups, divide the dough between two 6" cast-iron pans, and bake at 325 for 25-30 minutes for pizza cookies.
   b. For salted caramel cookies, increase the brown sugar to ¾ cup and salt to ½ tsp and scoop out twelve cookies.

Cowboy Cookies

Temp: 350°F   **Cook Time:** 18 min.

Ingredients:

- ½ cup butter, softened
- ½ cup brown sugar
- ½ cup sugar
- 1 egg, beaten
- 2 tsp vanilla extract
- 1 cup flour
- 1 cup rolled oats
- 1 tsp baking soda

- ½ tsp baking powder
- ½ tsp salt
- 1 cup chocolate chips
- 1 cup unsweetened shredded coconut
- ½ cup pecans
- ½ cup dried cranberries

Instructions:

1. Preheat oven to 350°F.
2. Cream butter and sugars in a large bowl and then add egg and vanilla.
3. Mix dry ingredients in a medium bowl.
4. Stir dry ingredients into wet ingredients, mixing until just combined.
5. Roll dough into twenty-four 2" balls or scoop with a cookie scoop.
6. Gently press the dough down to about 1" thick on a parchment-covered baking sheet.
7. Bake two sheets at a time for 10 minutes.
8. Rotate the cookie sheets top to bottom and front to back and bake for another 8 minutes.
9. Cookies should look slightly underdone when you remove them from the oven.
10. Cool for 10 minutes before serving.

Tippy and the Tomboy

She pushed off the pavement once more, and the *squeak…squeak* of her bike resumed its chorus down the shady street, joining the birds' twitter and scattering the squirrels in their chatter.

"Next house is three more up. Come on, Tippy!"

Tippy barked, scurrying to keep up with the squeaky bike. Joey smiled at her little dog, her white fur shining in the sunlight. She looks up, frowning at how far the sun has already risen, and quickens her peddling.

The morning had begun rather rushed. Well, to be fair, it started out not rushed with her not awake and not getting ready for her paper route. It then continued with her dad waking her, pushing her into the car before she could get ready, and heading to the man who handed out all the papers to all the delivery boys (and girls). Her dad was less than pleased, but both of them arrived in one piece and back in time for her to get her bike (and Tippy). *Sigh.*

Tippy's nails scratched the sidewalk, adding a nice percussion to their morning song, and they turned up the next driveway. Joey parked her bike and walked up to the door. She unadjusted her cap while Tippy came up to sit next to her, one ear cocked to the wooden door before them. Bag slung over her shoulder, uncombed hair, and slept-in clothes, the look was perfect, continuing the fable that most people assumed but never confirmed: she must be homeless, or at least an orphan. What mother would let their child leave the house like that? Hers, of course. But Joey didn't mind. It helped with tips, and so did Tippy.

A kind face paired with gray hair in curlers and plump shoulders in a bathrobe opened the door to the scene. Wide eyes looked up with anticipation, "Paper! Good morning. It is also payday, too." She sheepishly looked to Tippy.

"Oh, you sweet thing. Wait right here while I get your money."

Tippy smiled a lopsided grin up at her as the woman returned with what she owed, plus a little more. As she turned to continue with her morning, Joey heard one more, "That poor, poor thing," just before the door shut.

The scraggly pair returned to the bike and rode off down the driveway and onto the next street. Morning was already half over, the papers not half delivered, but the rest of the day was ahead of them.

"I wonder if Dad will take us fishing later today, Tippy?" Her pup gave a little bark.

"You're right. We'll just have to wait and see." Content with that thought, they raced their way from house to house, enjoying the sun and the perks of being a scraggly tomboy with her dog.

Oatmeal Cookies

Temp: 375°F

Cook Time: 9 min.

Ingredients:

- 2 cups rolled oats
- ⅓ cup water, hot
- 1 cup butter, melted
- ¼ cup sugar
- 1 cup brown sugar
- 1 tbl honey
- 1 tsp vanilla extract
- 2 eggs, beaten

- 2 cups flour
- ½ tbl ground cinnamon
- 1 tsp baking soda
- ½ tsp salt
- 1 cup dried cranberries (optional)
- 1 cup chocolate chips (optional)

Instructions:

1. In a small bowl, stir together oats with the hot water and set aside for 5 minutes.
2. Cream together butter and sugars in a large bowl. Add in vanilla and then the eggs. Do not over-mix.
3. In a separate bowl, mix the remaining dry ingredients, adding either the dried cranberries or chocolate chips if desired.
4. Add the dry ingredients to the wet ingredients, roll the dough into a 2" thick log in plastic wrap, and chill in the refrigerator for 1 hour. Or scoop out with a 2 tbl cookie scoop onto two parchment-lined baking sheets, cover, and chill.
5. Preheat oven to 375°F. Take the dough out of the refrigerator.
6. Cut dough into twenty-four 1" rounds and place 2" apart on two parchment-lined baking sheets.
7. Bake in oven for 9 minutes. You want the cookies to be soft.
8. Remove from oven and rest on pan for 5 minutes before moving to a cookie rack.

Peanut Butter Cookies

Temp: 350°F   **Cook Time:** 11 min.

Ingredients:

- 1 cup butter, softened
- 1 cup sugar
- ¾ cup brown sugar
- 2 eggs, beaten
- 2 tsp vanilla extract
- 1 cup peanut butter
- 3 cups flour

- 1 tsp baking soda
- 1 tsp baking powder
- ½ tsp salt

- Hershey kisses (optional)
- sugar (optional)

Instructions:

1. Cream butter and sugars together.
2. Mix in eggs, vanilla, and peanut butter.
3. In a separate bowl, mix dry ingredients.
4. Combine dry ingredients with wet ingredients.
5. Roll dough into 1 ½ -2" thick logs and cover in plastic wrap. Alternatively, scoop out with a large cookie scoop onto a parchment-lined baking sheet.
6. Refrigerate for 3 hours.
7. When you are ready to bake, preheat the oven to 350°F.
8. Cut logs into thirty-six 1" disks. You can either leave them in this shape or roll them into balls. If desired, roll in sugar.
9. Set dough onto parchment-lined baking sheets.
10. Bake for 11 minutes. Cookies should still be soft and only slightly brown when removed from the oven.
11. Let cookies set on the baking sheet for a few minutes before cooling on a cookie rack.
12. If desired, press a Hershey kiss into the center of each cookie.

Pecan Balls

Temp: 350°F

Cook Time: 10-12 min.

Ingredients:

- ½ cup butter, softened
- 1 ½ tsp vanilla extract
- ¼ cup powdered sugar
- ¼ tsp salt
- 1 cup flour
- ½ cup pecans, finely chopped
- ½ cup powdered sugar
- ⅓ cup chocolate chips, melted

Instructions:

1. Beat butter, vanilla, and powdered sugar until fluffy.
2. Stir in salt, flour, and pecans until just combined.
3. Cover and set in the refrigerator for 30 minutes.
4. Preheat oven to 350°F.
5. Use a 1 tbl cookie scoop to scoop out dough and roll it into 1" balls.
6. Set onto a parchment-covered baking sheet.
7. Bake for 10-12 minutes, or until they have set.
8. Roll warm cookies in powdered sugar and set aside to cool.
9. Melt chocolate in a small bowl in the microwave, stirring at 1 minute intervals until completely melted.
10. Roll cookies again in powdered sugar, drizzle in chocolate, and serve.

Shortbread Cookies

Temp: 375°F   **Cook Time:** 7-9 min.

Ingredients:

- 1 cup butter, softened
- ½ cup brown sugar
- 1 tsp vanilla extract
- 2 ¼ cups flour

- ½ cup sugar (optional)
- 1 tsp ground cinnamon (optional)

Instructions:

1. Combine butter, brown sugar, and vanilla in a large bowl.
2. Add flour and beat until the mixture forms a smooth, soft dough.
3. Divide dough in half and form two 2" thick logs.
4. Wrap in plastic wrap and refrigerate for 1-2 hours.
5. Preheat oven to 375°F.
6. Cut logs into twenty-four ¼" thick slices with a sharp knife.
   a. Alternatively, roll into balls and cover with cinnamon sugar.
7. Place 1" apart onto parchment-lined baking sheets.
8. Bake at 375°F for 7 to 9 minutes.
9. Remove from oven and cool for a few minutes before serving.

Spritz Cookies

Temp: 375°F   **Cook Time:** 13 min.

Ingredients:

- 1 egg, beaten
- 3 tsp vanilla extract
- 1 tbl heavy cream
- 1 cup butter, softened
- ⅔ cup sugar
- 2 ¼ cups flour
- ¼ tsp salt

Instructions:

1. Preheat oven to 375°F.
2. Combine egg, vanilla, cream, butter, and sugar in a medium bowl.
3. Mix in flour and salt until just combined.
4. Put the dough into a cookie press and press out cookies onto two parchment-lined baking sheets.
5. Place cookies in oven and bake for 13 minutes.
6. Remove from oven and let cookies set for a few minutes before serving.

Sugar Cookies

Temp: 375°F   **Cook Time:** 10 min.

Ingredients:

- ½ cup butter, softened
- 1 cup sugar
- 1 oz. cream cheese
- 2 tsp vanilla extract
- 1 tbl milk
- 1 egg, beaten

- 2 ¼ cups flour
- ½ tbl cornstarch
- ½ tsp baking powder
- ¼ tsp baking soda
- ½ tsp salt

Instructions:

1. Cream butter, sugar, and cream cheese with a mixer.
2. Beat in vanilla, milk, and egg.
3. Stir in the remaining ingredients and form a soft dough.
4. Divide dough in half and wrap balls in plastic wrap.
5. Refrigerate for 1 ½ hours or scoop out dough balls for immediate baking.
6. Preheat oven to 375°F.
7. Roll out dough to ¼-½" thick on a floured surface and cut out shapes with cookie cutters. Re-roll and cut out dough, placing each shape onto two parchment-lined baking sheets.
8. Bake in the oven for 10 minutes.
9. Cool on the baking sheet for 2 minutes and then set them on a cooling rack to finish.
10. Once fully cooled, decorate.

Cookie Frosting

Ingredients:

- 8 tbls butter, softened
- 2 cups powdered sugar
- 1 tsp vanilla extract
- food coloring

Instructions:

1. Beat ingredients in a medium bowl with a hand mixer.
2. Separate into smaller bowls before adding food coloring, adding just a drop at a time.
3. Use a spatula or butter knife to decorate cookies.

Cookie Icing

Ingredients:

- 2 ½ cups powdered sugar
- ½ tsp vanilla extract
- 4 tbls milk
- 1 tbl honey
- food coloring

Instructions:

1. Beat ingredients in a medium bowl with a hand mixer.
2. Separate into smaller bowls before adding food coloring, adding just a drop at a time.
3. Scrape into a piping bag with a small round tip for decorating.

Toffee Shortbread

Temp: 350°F   **Cook Time:** 15-20 min.

Ingredients:

- 1 cup flour
- ⅓ cup brown sugar
- 1 tsp vanilla extract
- 2 ½ tbls cornstarch
- ⅛ tsp salt
- ½ cup pecans
- ⅓ cup English toffee
- ½ cup butter, cold
- ½ cup chocolate chips, melted
- ¼ cup pecans, finely chopped

Instructions:

1. Preheat oven to 350°F.
2. In a food processor, combine flour, brown sugar, cornstarch, and salt.
3. Add pecans and toffee and process until finely chopped.
4. Add butter and vanilla, processing until it resembles a fine meal. This can also be done with a pastry cutter.
5. Scrape dough onto a floured counter and roll dough into a log about 4" in diameter.
6. Slice off ¼" thick cookies and place onto a parchment-lined baking sheet. With a sharp knife, cut each circle into quarters but do not separate.
7. Bake 15-20 minutes until cookies just begin to brown.
8. Cool for 2 minutes then cut through score marks to separate.
9. Once cool, dip the rounded edge of the wedges into melted chocolate and then into the chopped pecans.
10. Lay on wax or parchment paper to set.

Brownies

Temp: 350°F

Cook Time: 35 min.

Ingredients:

- 1 cup butter, melted
- ¼ cup chocolate chips
- 1 cup sugar
- 1 ¼ cups brown sugar
- ½ tsp salt
- 2 tsp vanilla extract
- 3 eggs, beaten
- 1 cup flour
- 1 cup cocoa powder
- ¾ cup chocolate chips

Instructions:

1. Preheat oven to 350°F.
2. Melt butter in a medium bowl. Whisk in ¼ cup chocolate chips.
3. Once the chips have melted, whisk in sugars, salt, and vanilla. Add eggs once the mixture has cooled.
4. Once wet ingredients are combined, stir in the remaining ingredients.
5. Line a 9x13" pan with parchment paper, leaving extra on the sides, and spray with pan spray.
6. Pour the batter into the pan and spread evenly.
7. Bake in the oven for 30 minutes. A toothpick should come out with some moist crumbs, not batter, when done. If it is not quite done, return to the oven for another 3-5 minutes.
8. Remove from oven and cool in pan before lifting and cutting.
   a. Alternatively, cut the recipe in half (1 egg), add to two 6" cast-iron pans, and bake for 15-20 minutes.

Coconut Bars

Ingredients:

- 4 cups unsweetened shredded coconut (7 oz)
- 2 cups powdered sugar
- 1 tsp vanilla extract
- 14 oz. sweetened condensed milk
- 2-4 cups chocolate chips
- 2-4 tsp coconut oil

Instructions:

1. In a medium bowl, mix coconut and powdered sugar. Then mix in sweetened condensed milk and vanilla.
2. Scrape the coconut mixture onto a wax paper-covered baking sheet and with wet hands press the coconut mixture to ½" thick. Place pan in the freezer for 4 hours.
3. In a separate medium to small bowl, slowly melt 2 cups of the chocolate chips in the microwave at 1 minute intervals between stirs or melt in a double boiler. Stir in 2 tsp of the coconut oil to form a thin chocolate.
4. Remove frozen coconut from the freezer and transfer it from wax paper to a cutting board.
5. Cut coconut into bar shapes, about 1"x3", or into squares.
6. Using two forks, dip coconut bars into the chocolate and set them back onto the wax paper.
7. Continue melting chocolate and coconut oil as needed.
8. Place bars in the refrigerator for 2 hours for the chocolate to set before serving. Store in the refrigerator.

Fruit Crumble Bars

Temp: 350°F   **Cook Time:** 40-45 min.

Ingredients:

- 1 cup flour
- 1 cup quick oats
- ¼ tsp baking soda
- ¼ tsp salt
- ½ cup brown sugar
- ½ cup butter, softened
- 1 cup fruit preserves, filling, or puree

Instructions:

1. Preheat oven to 350°F.
2. Combine dry ingredients in a large bowl.
3. Cut in butter to form a crumbly mixture.
4. Press ⅔ of the crumble mixture into a lightly greased 9x9" baking dish or pie dish.
5. Spread preserves on top and sprinkle with the remaining crumble mixture.
6. Bake for 40-45 minutes, or until golden.
7. Cool, cut into squares, and serve. Store in the refrigerator.

Honey Nut Snack Bars

Temp: 350°F   **Cook Time:** 15 min.

Ingredients:

- 2 cups rolled oats
- 1 cup unsweetened shredded coconut
- ½ cup almonds, chopped
- ½ cup cashews, chopped
- ½ cup walnuts, chopped
- ½ cup pecans, chopped
- ½ cup dates or prunes, chopped
- 1 ½ cups peanut butter
- 1 cup honey
- 1 tsp vanilla extract

Instructions:

1. Preheat oven to 350°F.
2. In a large bowl, combine dry ingredients.
3. In a small saucepan, combine peanut butter and honey at a low heat on the stove.
4. Add the vanilla to the wet mixture and stir.
5. Add to the oat mixture and stir until well combined.
6. Pour the mixture onto a greased baking sheet and press into a large rectangle about that is ½" thick.
7. Bake for 15 minutes until the edges barely turn brown.
8. Remove from oven and cool before cutting into bars.
9. Cut into to bars and store in the refrigerator.

No-bake Chocolate Berry Bars

Ingredients:

- ½ cup coconut oil
- ½ cup honey
- 1 tsp vanilla extract
- 1 ¼ cups chocolate chips
- 2 cups quick oats
- 1 cup unsweetened shredded coconut
- ⅔ cup dried cranberries or cherries

Instructions:

1. Melt coconut oil, honey, and vanilla in a medium saucepan at a low heat.
2. Turn off the heat and add chocolate chips, stirring until all have melted.
3. Once the chocolate chips have melted, mix in dry ingredients.
4. On a parchment-lined baking sheet, spread out the mixture to about ½" thick.
5. Set in the freezer for half an hour.
6. Cut into bars and store in the refrigerator.

Pecan Pie Bars

Temp: 350°F   **Cook Time:** 30 min.

Ingredients:

Crust

- 1 cup butter, softened
- ⅔ cup brown sugar
- 2 cups flour
- ½ tsp salt

Filling

- 1 ½ cup pecans
- ¼ tsp salt
- 4 tbls butter

- 1 cup chocolate chips

Caramel Sauce

- ½ cup butter, melted
- 1 cup brown sugar
- ¼ cup heavy cream
- ½ tsp salt
- ½ tbl vanilla extract

Instructions:

1. Preheat oven to 350°F and line a 9x13" baking dish with parchment paper. Spray with pan spray.
2. In a medium bowl, cream the butter and brown sugar. Stir in dry ingredients for the crust into the butter mixture.
3. Press the crust into the bottom of the dish. Place in fridge.
4. Toss pecans in ½ tsp of salt. Toast pecans in a fry pan at a medium heat for 4 minutes with 4 tbls butter.
5. Layer pecans over the crust and sprinkle with chocolate chips.
6. In a medium bowl, combine butter, brown sugar, and heavy cream. Return to microwave for 1 minute. Whisk in vanilla and salt.
7. Pour caramel sauce over chocolate and pecans.
8. Bake for 30 minutes until caramel bubbles around the edges.
9. Remove, cool for 1 hour until caramel sets, and cut to serve. Store in the refrigerator.

Seven-Layer Bars

Temp: 350°F   **Cook Time:** 25-30 min.

Ingredients:

- 12 graham cracker sheets
- ½ cup butter, melted
- 1 cup chocolate chips
- 1 cup butterscotch chips
- 1 cup sweetened shredded coconut
- 1 cup pecans, chopped
- 14 oz. sweetened condensed milk

Instructions:

1. Preheat oven to 350°F.
2. Crush graham crackers in a medium bowl and mix with melted butter.
3. Press crumbs into a parchment-lined 9x13" baking dish to form a crust.
4. Sprinkle chocolate chips, butterscotch chips, coconut, and pecans in four layers.
5. Pour sweetened condensed milk evenly over everything.
6. Place in oven and bake for 25-30 minutes, or until the coconut begins to look golden.
7. Remove from oven, cool, cut, and serve.

Cookie Truffles

Ingredients:

- 38 cream-filled cookies
- 8 oz. cream cheese, softened
- 24 oz. chocolate bark or chips, melted

Instructions:

1. Pulse sandwich cookies in a food processor until you have fine crumbs.
2. Add to a medium bowl and mix in cream cheese until fully combined.
3. Form forty 1" balls with a cookie scoop.
4. Set cookie balls on a parchment-lined baking sheet and refrigerate for 30 minutes.
5. Melt chocolate in a small bowl.
6. Dip cooled cookie balls in the chocolate with a fork and place them back on the baking sheet to set.
7. Drizzle coated truffles in more chocolate or sprinkle with cookie crumbs or chopped nuts.
8. Return to refrigerator to allow the chocolate to set before serving. These can be refrigerated for up to one week.

Hot Cheesecake

Temp: 350°F

Cook Time: 35 min.

Ingredients:

Dough

- ½ cup milk
- 2 ¼ tsp yeast
- 1 tbl sugar
- 2 ½ cups flour
- 1 cup butter, cold
- 3 egg yolks

Filling

- 32 oz. cream cheese
- 1 ½ cups sugar
- 2 egg yolks
- 2 tsp vanilla extract

- 2 tbls sugar

Instructions:

1. Begin making the dough by scalding and cooling the milk. Mix in yeast and sugar with the milk in a small bowl. Set it aside.
2. Cut butter into the flour in a medium bowl. Set it aside.
3. Add egg yolks to the milk, pour into the flour, and form a dough.
4. Divide the dough in half and wrap one half in plastic wrap.
5. Roll out one half of the dough on a floured surface into a 9x13" rectangle. Lay it into a greased 9x13" baking dish.
6. Beat together the filling ingredients and pour the mixture onto the dough.
7. Roll out the other half of the dough into a 9x13" rectangle on a floured surface. Lay it on top of the filling.
8. Sprinkle with 2 tbls sugar and rise for 1 hour.
9. Preheat oven to 350°F.
10. Bake for 30-35 minutes until the dough is golden.
11. Remove from oven and serve immediately.

Orange Slushie

"Pretty please?"

A pair of green eyes blinked into my own, a small lower lip barely stuck out to emphasize the desperation of one little eight-year-old heart.

"They only have them for this week, and I don't know when they will have them again, and they are my favorite, and it's not that far away, and…" the litany continued past my ability to listen. It was all the same, anyway. The reasons were numerous, the argument compelling, and all pointed to the same thing: the orange slushie was the only way to peace.

A frown crept across my face, and the creases between my brows led to a much smaller set of furrows on the little face before me. The pleading died down, but the face remained.

I looked out the window. Snow, sleet, and a fifteen-foot walk to the car stood before me. Who wanted a slushie midwinter? Slushies were for summertime, not when you may as well scoop one up from the sidewalk!

I listened as a whimper escaped the little lips now standing beside me, oblivious to the slow-moving cars driving past the house, whose occupants thought only of home and its warmth, anything but the misery about them. That same misery I was now contemplating.

The windshield wipers slogged away another mound of mush as my daughter slurped something of the same consistency, but orange, into her mouth. Hmph. I flexed my hands to get some feeling back into my fingers as they grew stiff around the cold steering wheel.

Home was still two blocks away, and the slushie was already half gone. How had she not gotten a brain freeze yet?

I glanced down at the little girl beside me. All the world was found in that orange slushie. The rain and snow did not matter. The cars slipping in the opposite lane did not matter. The cold in the car did not matter. The fact that I had just gotten home from work when the pleading began did not matter. Nothing but that orange slushie.

We pulled into the driveway and slipped to a stop. The slurping ceased.

"Hey, Dad?"

I grunted.

"Thanks for the slushie."

I looked at her as she finished the rest of that liquid gold. Contentment, accomplishment, and simple joy sat in that front seat. I smiled, and together we walked into our home.

Orange Jello Salad

Ingredients:

- 11 oz. mandarin oranges, drained
- 15 oz. crushed pineapple, drained
- 6 oz. orange jello mix
- 16 oz. cottage cheese
- 8 oz. whipped cream

Instructions:

1. Drain oranges and set aside ten slices for garnish.
2. Mix the well-drained oranges and pineapple with the jello mix.
3. Mix in cottage cheese and whipped cream.
4. Transfer to a serving bowl and garnish with oranges.
5. Refrigerate for 1 hour before serving.

Rice Pudding

Cook Time: 1 hr.

Ingredients:

- 3 cups water
- 1 ½ cups arborio rice
- 2 ½ cups half and half
- ¾ cup sugar
- ½ tsp salt
- 2 egg yolks
- 1 tsp vanilla extract
- ½ cup raisins
- whipped cream
- ground cinnamon

Instructions:

1. Bring water to a boil in a medium saucepan. Stir in rice, cover, and lower heat to simmer for 15 minutes, stirring occasionally, until the water is absorbed.
2. Remove from heat and set aside.
3. Add 1 ½ cups of the half and half along with the sugar and salt to a small saucepan and simmer for 5 minutes.
4. In a small bowl, mix the remaining half and half with the eggs, vanilla, and a ½ cup of the hot half and half.
5. Slowly pour and whisk the egg mixture into the saucepan and simmer for another 2 minutes.
6. Pour mixture over rice and stir together.
7. Heat rice pudding on medium for 10-15 minutes until it is thick and creamy, stirring continuously.
8. Remove from heat and stir in raisins. Allow to cool.
9. Spoon into dishes and top with whipped cream and cinnamon.

One Box Mud Buddies

Ingredients:

- 1 box square rice cereal (17 cups, 18 oz.)
- 1 ½ cups peanut butter
- 2 ½ cups chocolate chips
- 1 tsp vanilla extract
- 3 cups powdered sugar

Instructions:

1. Measure out cereal into a large bowl that has a lid.
2. In a small bowl, glass measuring cup, or saucepan, melt together peanut butter and chocolate chips, stirring occasionally so that the chocolate does not burn.
3. Stir vanilla into the chocolate mixture and pour over the cereal. Combine with a spatula until all is evenly covered.
4. Line a baking sheet with parchment paper and spread coated cereal evenly over the shcct.
5. Rest in the refrigerator for at least an hour until the chocolate is no longer warm and melty. You can skip this step and move straight to step 7, but you will need significantly more powdered sugar.
6. Remove from the refrigerator and return the cereal to the large bowl, breaking up any large pieces that have gotten stuck together.
7. Add powdered sugar, attach the lid to the bowl, and shake the bowl until the cereal is completely covered with powdered sugar.

Rice Crispies

Ingredients:

- 12 tbls butter
- 20 cups mini marshmallows (16 oz.=8 ½ cups, 10 oz.=6 cups)
- 1 tsp salt
- ½ tsp vanilla extract
- 11 cups rice cereal (12 oz. box)

Instructions:

1. Melt together butter and marshmallows in a large stockpot on medium-low.
2. Stir in salt and vanilla.
3. Remove from heat and stir in cereal.
4. Pour onto a parchment or wax paper-lined baking sheet.
5. Wet hands and press cereal flat to a ½"-1" thickness.
6. Cool for at least 1 hour before cutting into squares.

Caramel Corn

Temp: 250°F

Cook Time: 1 hr.

Ingredients:

- ⅓ cup popcorn kernels (8 cups popped)
- olive oil
- ½ cup butter
- 1 cup brown sugar
- ½ tsp salt
- 1 tsp vanilla extract
- ¼ tsp baking soda
- ½ cup chocolate chips, melted (optional)
- ½ cup nuts (optional)

Instructions:

1. Preheat oven to 250°F.
2. Pour a thin layer of olive oil into the bottom of a large stock pot, just enough to coat the bottom. Place three kernels in the bottom, put on the lid, and turn the stove to medium. Wait for the kernels to pop before adding the rest of the popcorn.
3. Once popped, set popcorn aside in a large bowl. Add nuts if desired.
4. Melt butter and brown sugar in a medium saucepan.
5. Raise heat to medium-high and simmer for 5 minutes.
6. Remove from heat and stir in salt, vanilla, and baking soda.
7. Pour the caramel mixture over the popcorn and stir together with a rubber spatula to coat evenly.
8. Spread popcorn onto a parchment-lined baking sheet and place in the oven for 1 hour. Stir the popcorn every 15 minutes to make sure it is cooking evenly.
9. Remove from oven and cool completely before serving. If desired, drizzle with melted chocolate.

Oh, the Places You'll Go

Perhaps you are like me and tend to stress clean. There's something on your mind, something you can't deal with yet or can't control, so you clean. You reorder the spaces around you, your life, so that perhaps maybe, maybe, you can think clearly again. Or maybe you're a little ADD, like my husband, who can start one thing, intending it to only take a minute or two, and end up going through that book that hey, you haven't seen this in FOREVER! and have to look at it right now and before you know it, the day is half gone. Or maybe you're like this old dog I had, Bella, who was as distractable as all get out. Food? Car? Duck? Squirrel? It'd take only seconds, but the tasks would change just as quickly.

This is what I thought about as I cleaned the walls the other day. They had needed cleaning for weeks (months) now and I'd just about had it and decided to get to it. So, I cleaned the walls by the base of the stairs and made my way up, foot by foot, step by step, until I reached the top. That was when I realized that I needed to also wash the wall at the top of the stairs and as I made my way around the hallway to the doorframe of the bathroom, I noticed that it had clearly been weeks (months) since I'd taken care of the hair and dust and who-knows-what-else along the edge of the tile floor. So, I set down my magic eraser (I sometimes think it is truly magic) to get the vacuum. The vacuuming went faster than expected, so I decided to get a washcloth and wash the tile as well and snag a couple of the cobwebs that had formed in the corners. But on my way back through the hallway, I saw a little trail of crumbs along the floor runner. Well, I already had the vacuum out, but I could not start in the hallway (obviously). I had to start in our bedroom and work my way out. I was startled by the rattling making its way up the body of the cleaner, as I

283

was sure it had only been days (weeks?) since I'd last vacuumed up here. I finished on the other side of the bed and observed my work as I rolled the vacuum back to the hallway. As it was just the runner, this stretch went fairly smoothly, until I walked past the baby's bedroom door. My nose noticed that the trash clearly had not been taken out y—oh my goodness, it is MONDAY. I raced down the stairs (with the trashcan), vaulted out the door, and brought it to the edge of the road just as the truck rolled past. Great. As I carried it back to the porch, I noticed that the leaves from last Fall were still huddled in the corner by my office. Well, if I can't get the trash done, at least I can finish the porch. Shutting the door behind me, I was able to notice the complete silence of the house, which was odd considering I had two small children. After a brief search, I found them playing cheerfully with the chapstick. Could be worse, but at least it was finally nap time. This proved to be little struggle, until I realized half the struggle was playing with the vacuum. But this was sweet, as she was merely copying me from minutes (an hour) before. I smiled, tucked them into bed, and headed downstairs.

I was tired at this point, with the chores half done and barely anything to show for it. But it was time for a break (and a snack) but what to do? Well, cookies were too complicated, bread too late, and my time was rapidly running short. So, as I finished the dishes, I came across a mug, my second favorite mug. My first favorite mug is for hot chocolate, but this mug, oh this mug. This mug was the size of a small bowl, perfect for hot chocolate, tea, chili, soup, and, best of all, brownies. Yes, I thought as I dried the last dish, a mug brownie was in order. So, in a few brief minutes, I whisked the ingredients together, warmed them up to gooey goodness, and settled in with my Nessie spoon and a book. I had barely finished the last bite and turned a page when I heard stirrings above me. But that was ok. I'd had a few moments of peace with my brownie and my book. *What's not to love?* I thought as I ran my hand up the banister, which my goodness, when was this last washed? Months ago? (It had been at least a year. Oh, there's my magic eraser.) But I would get to it, sometime after getting my favorite baby snuggles.

Where was I going with this? Who knows. I know I certainly don't. My mind jumps from one thing to the next when I am stressed (and hungry). So, if you find yourself in this position, take a moment to breathe. Put those littles to bed, set your washcloth down, find your favorite (or second favorite) mug, and make yourself a personal, gooey, perfect brownie. You will thank me (and yourself) for having taken a moment from all those places you go.

Mug Brownie

Cook Time: 1:15 min.

Ingredients:

- 2 tbls butter
- 2 tbls brown sugar
- ½ tbl sugar
- ½ tsp vanilla extract
- ⅛ tsp salt
- 2 tbls cocoa powder
- 2 tbls flour
- 2 tbls milk
- 2 tbls chocolate chips

Instructions:

1. Melt butter in a large mug or small glass bowl.
2. Stir in sugars, vanilla, and salt.
3. Stir in cocoa powder then flour.
4. Stir in milk then chocolate chips (you do not want the chocolate chips to melt before baking).
5. Once everything is combined, cook in the microwave for 1 minute and 15 seconds, or 1 minute and 20 seconds at the most. If you want a super gooey brownie, bake for 1 minute.
6. Remove, cool for a few minutes, and eat with a scoop of vanilla ice cream.

Mug Cookie

Cook Time: 60 seconds

Ingredients:

- 2 tbls butter
- 1 tbl brown sugar
- 1 tbl 1 tsp sugar
- ¼ tsp vanilla extract
- ⅛ tsp salt
- 1 tbl milk
- ⅓ cup flour
- ⅛ tsp baking soda
- 2 tbls chocolate chips

Instructions:

1. Soften butter in a large mug or small glass bowl.
2. Stir in sugars, vanilla, and salt.
3. Stir in milk then flour and baking soda.
4. Stir in chocolate chips.
5. Once everything is combined, add to the microwave for 60 seconds.
6. Remove, cool for a few minutes, and eat with a scoop of vanilla ice cream.

Hot Fudge

Cook Time: 5 min.

Ingredients:

- ½ cup butter
- 1 cup brown sugar
- ½ tsp salt
- 1 cup heavy cream
- 1 tsp vanilla extract
- 1 cup chocolate chips

Instructions:

1. Melt butter in a small saucepan and add sugar and salt.
2. Bring to a simmer, not a boil or it will crystallize.
3. Turn off the heat and stir in heavy cream and vanilla.
4. Stir in chocolate chips.
5. Pour into a jar and serve. Store in refrigerator.

Caramel Topping

Cook Time: 5 min.

Ingredients:

- ½ cup butter
- 1 cup brown sugar
- 1 tsp salt
- 1 cup heavy cream
- 1 tsp vanilla extract

Instructions:

1. Melt butter in a small saucepan and add sugar and salt.
2. Bring to a simmer, not a boil or it will crystallize.
3. Turn off the heat and stir in heavy cream and vanilla.
4. Pour into a jar and serve. Store in refrigerator.

Hot Chocolate

Ingredients:

- 2 ½ tbls cocoa powder
- ½ tsp ground cinnamon
- 1 ½ tbls sugar
- ½ tsp vanilla extract
- ½ cup heavy cream
- ¾ cup milk

Instructions:

1. Add cocoa, cinnamon, sugar, and vanilla to a small saucepan.
2. Pour in cream and milk.
3. Turn the stove on to a medium heat.
4. Whisk ingredients together until they show a little frothiness.
5. Continue to stir and simmer until it begins to rise in the pan.
6. Immediately remove from heat and pour into a large mug.
7. Top with whipped cream or marshmallows and serve with shortbread or wafer cookies.

Lemonade

Ingredients:

- 1 ¾ cups white sugar
- 1 ½ cups lemon juice
- 8 cups water

Instructions:

1. In a small saucepan, combine sugar and 1 cup of water.
2. Bring to a boil, stirring to dissolve sugar.
3. Allow to cool to room temperature and refrigerate.
4. In a large pitcher, stir chilled sugar water, lemon juice, and the remaining 7 cups of water.

Polish Desserts

A Christmas Surprise

This mission was clear, the route set. Though there would be many obstacles, the goal would make the adventure worthwhile. It was time to find the Christmas gifts.

Joey crossed her arms and tapped her foot, her eyes roaming the different entryways to the rest of the house. The tree was still empty of gifts underneath. Perhaps she should start in the basement? It was not a great place to visit, crowded with the collections of years and impulses. That might be a good place to hide gifts. She moved quietly through the kitchen, but just as she turned to the stairs, she stopped. No, that is where all the Christmas supplies were. That would be the first place she would look, so he could not have hidden it there.

She turned around and walked back to the hallway. They would not be in her brother's room, and it definitely wasn't in hers (she'd already checked). That left only the hall closet and her parents' room. Cautiously, she opened the closet and peered in. But she wasn't careful enough. Empty boxes and crumpled linens tumbled onto the floor before she had the time to catch them. Cramming everything back in, Joey closed the door. Of course not. Mom put too many things in there to make it a good hiding place. Their bedroom it is!

Noticing the room was already open, Joey snuck in and looked around. She did not think her dad would have hidden any gifts in the drawers, overflowing as they were. She crouched down. Nope, nothing but dust bunnies under the bed. That left only Dad's closet.

The door was tough to open, but it finally budged past the floor's obstacles. A smile lit her face. Tucked behind a shoebox was a hint of red and green. Grunting, she reached as far as she could, but she just wasn't tall enough. Backing up, she looked around the room and saw a chair. Balancing on it precariously, the box was now within reach. It was small, filling only her two hands.

Joey paused a moment, making sure no one was listening, and shook the box. Something thumped against the insides of the box. It did not rattle, or chime, or do much of anything. It was too light for a book, not that her dad would have gotten that for her anyway. It was too small to be sports equipment. Perhaps a camera?

Rotating the box, she found where the wrapping paper had been taped shut. The temptation was too great, the desire to know too strong! And the skill of a child who had to know made it all the more tempting. Christmas was simply too far away to wait and find out the contents. Breathing softly on the tape, Joey watched as the moisture loosened the paper from its binds. Ever so gently, she pulled apart each piece of tape and unfolded every crease. Within was a box, but unmarked. She would have to dig deeper.

Curiosity getting the better of her, Joey opened the side flap. Slowly, she turned the side of the box and let its prize fall into her hands. It was a calculator. She stared at it for a moment, running her hand over its cover, and a tear ran from her eye. Wiping it away, she marveled at this special gift. This was not any calculator, but the one she specifically needed for her class, the one that would help her meet her dreams to make it to Wall Street, further than anyone else had gone, and that next step lay in her hands.

She sniffed, rubbed her eyes, and put the brand-new calculator back into the box, closing the side flap. Carefully, she refolded the wrapping paper around the cardboard, laying the tape ever so gently back down, resealing the precious gift inside. She climbed back onto the chair, snuck the gift back behind the shoebox, and closed the door. Joey went back to her room and laid down on her bed, looking at the ceiling as she considered this wonderful gift her dad had wanted to surprise her with, the surprise now ruined. It was the exact model she had asked for, and another tear threatened to escape.

She shook her head. It would still be a surprise, and she would show her dad just how thankful she was in just a couple more weeks. She would find it for the first time under the tree, shake the box, and guess at its contents. Maybe it was a game, or something to grow in the garden? He would show a small smile and say no, open it already! And she would tear the paper off with little grace, forcing the cardboard open, and shout with delight at the calculator within, a surprise for everyone. It would be an adventure for sure, but the goal would make the obstacles and wait worthwhile. For in the end, she would not just have a calculator but a small smile from Dad, who got a surprise gift for his little girl.

Chruściki (Angel Wings)

Temp: 350°F   **Cook Time:** 30 min.

Ingredients:

- 4 egg yolks
- ¼ cup sugar
- ¼ tsp salt
- 1 tsp vanilla extract
- 4 tbls heavy cream
- 1 tbl rum, or vinegar
- ¼ tsp lemon juice

- 1 ⅓ cups flour
- canola oil
- powdered sugar

Instructions:

1. Beat egg yolks, sugar, and salt in a mixing bowl on high for 1 minute to form a thick mixture.
2. Stir vanilla, cream, rum, and lemon juice into the mixture.
3. Add flour slowly to form a soft dough.
4. Knead for a couple more minutes on a floured surface.
5. Cover and rest for 10 minutes.
6. Heat 2" of oil to 350°F in a medium saucepan.
7. Cut the dough in half. Wrap one half in plastic wrap and set aside.
8. Roll out dough onto a floured surface to no more than ⅛".
9. Cut dough into 1x4" strips and slit each diagonally.
10. Pull one end of the strip through the slit to make a twisted shape.
11. Once you have prepared all the dough, fry chruściki for 15 seconds on each side, remove, and drain on a paper towel.
12. Once dry, dust with powdered sugar and serve.

Ciasto Trzech Króli
(ThreeKingsCake)

Temp: 325°F   **Cook Time:** 45-60 min.

Ingredients:

- 1 ½ cups butter, softened
- 1 ½ cups brown sugar
- 1 cup sugar
- 6 eggs, beaten
- 2 tsp vanilla extract
- 1 ½ cups brandy or eggnog
- ½ cup raisins
- ¾ cup dates or dried apricots, chopped
- 1 cup walnuts, chopped
- 3 ½ cups flour
- 1 tsp baking powder
- ½ tsp salt
- 1 silver or chocolate coin
- ¼ cup powdered sugar

Instructions:

1. Preheat oven to 325°F and grease a Bundt pan and a 9x5" bread pan.
2. Cream butter and sugars in a large bowl.
3. Mix in eggs, vanilla, and eggnog.
4. Whisk dry ingredients in a medium bowl and toss with nuts and dried fruit.
5. Stir dry ingredients slowly into wet ingredients and stir until just combined.
6. Pour into Bundt pan and bread pan. Place a clean silver coin or chocolate coin into the batter in the Bundt pan.
7. Bake for 45-60 minutes, or until the cake is springy.
8. Remove from oven and cool.
9. Invert Bundt cake onto a plate and dust with powdered sugar.

Kołaczki

Temp: 375°F

Cook Time: 12-15 min.

Ingredients:

- 3 cups flour
- ½ tsp salt
- 1 cup butter, cold
- 6 oz. cream cheese
- 2 egg yolks, beaten

- 2 tsp vanilla extract
- 1 cup fruit preserves
- ½ cup powdered sugar

Instructions:

1. Combine flour and salt with butter using a pastry blender.
2. Form into a dough with cream cheese, yolks, and vanilla.
3. Divide dough into four portions, wrap, and chill in the refrigerator for 1 hour.
4. Preheat oven to 375°F.
5. Roll out dough ⅛" thick on a floured surface.
6. To make the cookies:
   a. Cut the dough into 3" squares or circles, place 1 tsp of preserves into the center, wet one corner, and fold over the opposite corner in the center of the cookie and press together.
   b. Or, roll the dough to ¼" thick, cut out 2" circles, press your thumb into the dough to make a bowl, and fill it with 1 tsp of preserves.
7. Place these onto a parchment-lined baking sheet.
8. Bake for 12-15 minutes or until golden.
9. Remove from oven, cool, and dust with powdered sugar.

Paczki

Temp: 375°F; 360°F   **Cook Time:** 10 min; 30 min.

Ingredients:

- 2 ¼ tsp instant yeast
- ⅓ cup white sugar
- 1 cup milk, warmed
- 3 tbls butter, melted
- 3 egg yolks, beaten
- ½ tsp vanilla extract
- ½ tsp salt
- 3 ½ cups flour

- powdered sugar
- 2 tbls butter, melted
- ⅓ cup sugar

- 2 cups filling (custard, fruit, or creme)

- canola oil

Instructions:

1. Proof yeast in milk and sugar for 10 minutes.
2. Stir in butter, yolks, vanilla, and salt.
3. Mix in flour to form a soft but somewhat sticky dough.
4. Knead for 5 minutes on a floured surface. The dough should be soft and elastic when you are finished.
5. Cover and rest in a warm place for 45 minutes. Make filling.
6. Roll out dough on a floured surface to ½" thick.
7. Cut out circles with a 3" floured biscuit cutter.
8. Place circles onto a parchment-lined baking sheet, cover, and rise for 35 minutes until they have doubled in size.
9. Preheat oven to 375°F or heat up 2" of oil to 360°F.
10. Bake for 10 minutes in the oven, or fry in oil until each side is golden, about 20 seconds per side.
11. Dust in powdered sugar or brush with butter and toss in sugar.
12. Fill a small-tipped pastry bag with your filling of choice, push the tip into the side of the paczki, and fill slowly.

Pierniczki (Gingerbread Cookies)

Temp: 350°F

Cook Time: 8-10 min.

Ingredients:

- ½ cup honey
- ¼ cup butter
- ½ cup dark brown sugar
- 2 eggs, beaten
- 1 tsp baking soda
- 2 tbls milk
- ½ tsp vanilla extract

- 2 tsp ground cinnamon
- 2 tsp ground ginger
- 1 tsp cocoa powder
- ½ tsp ground cloves
- ¼ tsp ground nutmeg
- ½ tsp salt
- 3 cups flour

Instructions:

1. Melt honey, butter, and brown sugar together in a medium saucepan.
2. Remove from heat and cool.
3. Beat eggs in a small bowl and stir into the cooled mixture.
4. Stir baking soda into milk and add to the mixture.
5. In a medium bowl, stir together spices and flour.
6. Add liquid ingredients to the dry ingredients and mix to form a thick dough.
7. Shape into a ball, cover with plastic wrap, and refrigerate for 30 minutes.
8. Preheat oven to 350°F.
9. Roll out on a floured surface to ¼" thick.
10. Cut out shapes and place them on a parchment-lined baking sheet.
11. Bake for 8-10 minutes until the edges begin to brown.
12. Remove, cool, and serve, or decorate with melted chocolate or icing.

Makowiec (Poppy Seed Roll)

Temp: 350°F

Cook Time: 35 min.

Ingredients:

Filling

- 1 ½ cups poppy seeds
- ¼ cup raisins, pureed
- ¼ cup walnuts, chopped
- ½ cup milk, hot
- ¾ cup sugar
- 2 tbls butter, melted
- ½ tsp lemon juice
- 1 tsp vanilla extract
- 1 egg, beaten

Dough

- 3 tsp yeast
- ⅔ cup milk, warm
- ⅓ cup butter, softened
- 2 eggs, beaten
- 3 ½ cups flour
- ¼ cup sugar
- ½ tsp salt

Glaze

- 1 cup powdered sugar
- 2 tbls milk

Instructions:

1. Grind poppy seeds in a food processor until they are moist.
2. In a medium bowl, combine seeds, raisins, nuts, and milk.
3. In a stand mixer, proof yeast in milk for 10 minutes.
4. Add remaining dough ingredients. Knead for 5 minutes into a soft dough. Cover the dough and rest for 10 minutes.
5. Add the remaining filling ingredients to poppy seed mixture.
6. Roll out dough into a 12" square and spread filling evenly across the dough, leaving a border.
7. Roll into a log and pinch off the ends. Set the roll on a parchment-covered baking sheet to rise for 1 ½ hours.
8. Preheat oven to 350°F.
9. Bake poppy seed roll for 35 minutes. Meanwhile, mix glaze.
10. Remove from oven, cool, and drizzle with glaze.

Rugelach

Temp: 375°F   **Cook Time:** 15-17 min.

Ingredients:

- 2 ¾ cups flour
- ¼ cup sugar
- ½ tsp salt
- 1 cup butter, cold
- 6 oz. cream cheese
- 2 tsp vanilla extract
- 2 egg yolks

- 1 cup preserves
- ½ cup powdered sugar

Filling

- 1 cup chocolate chips, minced
- 1 cup walnuts, minced
- 1 tbl ground cinnamon
- ¼ cup brown sugar

Instructions:

1. Combine flour, sugar, salt, and butter with a pastry blender.
2. Combine flour mixture with cream cheese, vanilla, and yolks into a dough.
3. Divide dough into four portions, wrap, and set in the refrigerator for 1 hour.
4. Combine the filling ingredients in a small bowl.
5. Preheat oven to 375°F.
6. Roll out each portion into a 10" circle ⅛" thick on a lightly floured surface.
7. Spread a layer of preserves onto each dough circle and sprinkle with filling.
8. Cut each circle into 16 wedges using a pastry or pizza cutter.
9. Roll each wedge from base to the point.
10. Place cookies point down on a parchment-lined baking sheet.
11. Bake for 15-17 minutes, or until golden.
12. Remove from oven and dust with powdered sugar.

Sugar-Free Rugelach

Temp: 375°F

Cook Time: 15-17 min.

Ingredients:

- 2 ¾ cups flour
- 1 cup butter, cold
- 8 oz. cream cheese
- 2 tsp vanilla extract
- 1 cup apricot preserves

Filling

- 1 cup raisins, minced
- 1 cup walnuts, minced
- 2 tbls ground cinnamon

Instructions:

1. Combine flour and butter with a pastry blender.
2. Combine flour mixture with cream cheese and vanilla into a dough.
3. Divide dough into four portions, wrap, and set in the refrigerator for 1 hour.
4. Combine the filling ingredients in a small bowl.
5. Preheat oven to 375°F.
6. Roll out each portion into a 10" circle ⅛" thick on a lightly floured surface.
7. Spread a layer of preserves onto each dough circle and sprinkle with filling.
8. Cut each circle into 16 wedges using a pastry or pizza cutter.
9. Roll each wedge from base to the point.
10. Place cookies point down on a parchment-lined baking sheet.
11. Bake for 15-17 minutes, or until golden.
12. Remove from oven and serve.

Sernik (Cheesecake)

Temp: 350°F   **Cook Time:** 1 hr. 30 min.

Ingredients:

- 1 cup flour
- ½ cup sugar
- ½ cup butter, cold
- 2 eggs, beaten
- 3 tbls sour cream

Toppings

- powdered sugar, fruit preserves, caramel, or chocolate

Filling

- 2 lbs. farmer's cheese or cream cheese
- 1 ½ cups sugar
- 2 tsp vanilla extract
- 1 tbl flour
- 1 cup heavy cream
- ½ cup raisins (optional)
- 5 eggs, separated

Instructions:

1. Blend flour, sugar, and butter in a large bowl. Mix in eggs and sour cream. If the dough is too dry or wet, add 1 tbl of water or flour accordingly.
2. Press dough into the bottom of a 10" springform pan, cover with plastic wrap, and set in the refrigerator for 20 minutes.
3. Preheat oven to 350°F.
4. Cube farmer's cheese and blend smooth in a pastry blender.
5. Mix cheese, sugar, vanilla, flour, cream, and raisins in a bowl.
6. Separate the eggs, mixing yolks into the cheese mixture. Beat whites to soft peaks, then mix into cheese until just combined.
7. Uncover the crust and bake for 15 minutes.
8. Remove from oven, add cheese mixture, and bake for 1 hour. If the top browns too quickly, cover it with foil.
9. When the middle is barely jiggly, turn off the oven and leave the pan in for 30 minutes. Remove, cool, and add toppings.

Family Recipes

Temp: **Cook Time:**

Ingredients:

-
-
-
-
-
-
-
-

Instructions:

1.
2.
3.
4.
5.
6.
7.
8.

Temp: **Cook Time:**

Ingredients:

-
-
-
-
-
-
-
-

Instructions:

1.
2.
3.
4.
5.
6.
7.
8.

Temp: **Cook Time:**

Ingredients:

-
-
-
-
-
-
-
-

Instructions:

1.
2.
3.
4.
5.
6.
7.
8.

Temp: **Cook Time:**

Ingredients:

-
-
-
-
-
-
-
-

Instructions:

1.
2.
3.
4.
5.
6.
7.
8.

Temp: **Cook Time:**

Ingredients:

-
-
-
-
-
-
-
-

Instructions:

1.
2.
3.
4.
5.
6.
7.
8.

Temp: **Cook Time:**

Ingredients:

-
-
-
-
-
-
-
-

Instructions:

1.
2.
3.
4.
5.
6.
7.
8.

Temp: **Cook Time:**

Ingredients:

-
-
-
-
-
-
-
-

Instructions:

1.
2.
3.
4.
5.
6.
7.
8.

Temp: **Cook Time:**

Ingredients:

-
-
-
-
-
-
-
-

Instructions:

1.
2.
3.
4.
5.
6.
7.
8.

Temp: **Cook Time:**

Ingredients:

-
-
-
-
-
-
-
-

Instructions:

1.
2.
3.
4.
5.
6.
7.
8.

Temp: **Cook Time:**

Ingredients:

-
-
-
-
-
-
-
-

Instructions:

1.
2.
3.
4.
5.
6.
7.
8.

Temp: **Cook Time:**

Ingredients:

-
-
-
-
-
-
-
-

Instructions:

1.
2.
3.
4.
5.
6.
7.
8.

Temp: **Cook Time:**

Ingredients:

-
-
-
-
-
-
-
-

Instructions:

1.
2.
3.
4.
5.
6.
7.
8.

Kitchen Extras

Quick Bites for Little Mouths

Try as I might, I have picky kids. Or maybe it's just a stage? Either way, these are some little recipes that use up extra things or are easy to make for kids to eat. Enjoy!

Pancakes:

- 1 cup plain yogurt
- 1 cup flour
- ½ cup milk
- 2 tsp baking powder
- 1 cup blueberries
- 2 tbls sugar

1. Mix ingredients and pour ¼ cup of batter onto a greased pan.
2. Bake for about 2 minutes on each side, or until you see bubbles and they have turned golden.
3. Remove from pan, cool, and serve.

Baked Oatmeal:

- ⅓ cup quick oats
- ⅓ cup milk/water
- 1 egg
- ¼ tsp ground cinnamon
- 1 ½ tbls honey (after 1 year old)
- ¼ cup blueberries

1. Mix all ingredients in a microwave-safe bowl or glass dish.
2. Cook in the microwave for 3 minutes until the center is no longer gooey.
3. Remove, chop up and cool, and serve.

French Toast Sticks:

- 4 hot dog buns
- 4 eggs
- ½ cup half and half
- 1 tsp vanilla extract
- butter
- 2 tbls sugar
- 1 tbl ground cinnamon

1. Cut each half of the hot dog buns into 5 pieces.
2. Mix eggs, half and half, and vanilla in a wide, shallow dish.
3. Heat a frypan to a medium heat and coat with butter.
4. Dip bun pieces into the egg mixture and fry in butter. Each side should only take a minute. Remove from heat and set on a paper towel.
5. Mix cinnamon and sugar, dust French toast pieces, and serve.

Corn Dogs:

- 4 hot dogs
- ½ cup cornmeal
- ⅓ cup water
- ½ cup pancake mix

Scratch pancake mix:
- ½ cup flour
- 1 tsp baking powder
- 1 ½ tbls sugar
- ¼ tsp salt

- olive or canola oil

1. Cut hot dogs into 1" pieces.
2. Mix cornmeal, pancake mix, and water to form a thick batter.
3. Heat 1" of cooking oil in a small saucepan to 330°F.
4. Dip hot dogs into batter and fry each side in oil until golden.
5. Drain, cool, and serve.

Pita Pizza:

- 1 pita
- 2 tbls pizza sauce
- 2 tbls cheddar cheese, shredded
- ¼ cup mozzarella cheese, shredded
- 4 pepperoni

1. Spread sauce on the pita, leaving a ½" on the edge.
2. Add cheese and pepperoni.
3. Cook in a toaster oven on high for 8-10 minutes, the oven at 400°F for 8 minutes, or in a frypan until the cheese is melted.
4. Cut and serve.

Mini Mac & Cheese:

- ⅓ cup macaroni noodles
- ⅔ cup water
- ⅛ tsp salt
- 2 tbls milk
- ⅓ cup cheddar cheese, shredded
- ½ tbl butter

1. Boil macaroni in a medium dish with water for 5 minutes in the microwave, stirring occasionally.
2. Add all ingredients to a small bowl and stir together.
3. Melt for 1 ½ minutes, stirring occasionally, and serve.

Barbecue Meatballs:

- 12 cooked meatballs
- ⅓ cup brown sugar
- ⅓ cup barbecue sauce
- 1 tbl water

1. Melt and stir together brown sugar, barbecue sauce, and water in a small saucepan for 3 minutes at a medium heat.
2. Add meatballs and continue to stir together until meatballs are warm and serve.

Sweet Potato Bars:

- 1 cup sweet potato (1 medium potato)
- 1 cup rolled oats
- ½ tsp ground cinnamon
- 1 tbl honey (optional)

1. Wash sweet potatoes, poke holes in them, wrap them in foil, and bake them on a baking sheet in the oven at 450°F for at least 1 hour, or until they are soft when you stick a fork in them. Remove and cool.
2. Peel off the skin and blend smooth in a food processor.
3. Add the rolled oats, cinnamon, and honey, if desired.
4. Blend either until just combined or the oats are processed.
5. Spread onto a parchment-lined baking sheet and bake in the oven at 375°F for 20 minutes.
6. Remove, cool, cut, and serve.

Fruit and Cheerio Bars:

- 3 cups cheerios
- 1 cup dried cranberries
- ½ cup quick oats
- ¼ tsp ground cinnamon
- 4 cups mini marshmallows
- 4 tbls butter
- ¼ tsp vanilla extract

1. In a medium bowl, stir together dry ingredients.
2. In a small saucepan, melt butter and marshmallows.
3. Stir for 2 minutes, then remove from heat and add vanilla.

4. Combine wet and dry ingredients.
5. Press the cheerio mixture into a parchment-lined 9x13" baking dish and place in the refrigerator for 2 hours to set.
6. Cut and serve.

Deep-fried Oreos:

- 6 double-stuffed Oreos
- ½ cup pancake mix
- ¼ cup water or milk
- canola oil

Scratch pancake mix:
- o ½ cup flour
- o 1 tsp baking powder
- o 1 ½ tbls sugar
- o ¼ tsp salt

1. Add 2" of canola oil to a small saucepan and heat to a medium-high heat, about 330°F.
2. In a small bowl, combine pancake mix with enough water to form a thick pancake batter.
3. Dip Oreos into pancake mix and gently set into canola oil, but no more than two or three at a time so they do not touch.
4. After a minute, turn over with tongs so the other side will fry to a golden color.
5. Remove from the oil and drain on a paper towel.
6. Serve with ice cream.

Peanut Butter Cups:

- ½ cup peanut butter
- 4-5 tbls powdered sugar
- 1 cup chocolate

1. Blend peanut butter and powdered sugar.
2. Spoon into 6 cupcake liners resting in a muffin pan or into a small pie tin.

3. Melt the chocolate slowly, stirring every 30 seconds. If you overheat the chocolate, add a bit of coconut oil.
4. Spoon chocolate on top of peanut butter.
   a. Or coat the bottom of the liners with chocolate, freeze, add peanut butter, and top with chocolate.
5. Set in refrigerator to cool. Once the chocolate has set, serve.

Saltine Toffee:

- 24 saltines
- 1 cup butter
- 1 cup brown sugar
- 1 ⅓ cups chocolate chips

1. Lay saltines on a parchment-covered 9x13" pan.
2. In a small mixing bowl, melt butter and brown sugar in the microwave for 3 minutes, mixing every 30 seconds.
3. Spread evenly over saltines and bake in the oven or toaster oven for 6 minutes at 400°F.
4. Top with chocolate chips and let them sit for 5 minutes.
5. Smooth chocolate chips evenly, add other desired toppings, and refrigerate for 2 hours.
6. Break apart and serve once the chocolate has set.

Popcorn:

- olive oil
- popcorn kernels
- butter
- salt

1. Take a pot with a lid and add just enough olive oil to coat the bottom. Add three popcorn kernels.
2. Place the lid on the pot and turn the heat on the stove to medium. When the kernels pop, add enough kernels to cover the bottom of the pot without crowding.

3. Replace the lid, holding it askew, and rock the pot on the burner as the popcorn pops. When you hear no more popping, remove from heat and pour into a bowl.
4. Add butter to the bottom of the pot and, once melted, add to popcorn and toss with salt.

Blueberry Crumble:

- 2 tbls sugar
- 2 tbls brown sugar
- ¾ cup flour
- ¼ tsp baking powder
- ¼ tsp salt
- ⅓ cup butter, softened
- ½ tsp lemon juice

- ¼ tsp vanilla extract
- 1 ½ tbls water

- 1 cup blueberries
- 2 tbls sugar
- 1 tsp cornstarch
- ⅛ tsp ground cinnamon

1. Preheat oven or toaster oven to 350°F.
2. Whisk sugars, flour, baking powder, and salt in a small bowl.
3. Combine with butter, lemon juice, vanilla, and water into a crumbly dough.
4. Press half of the dough into an 8" square baking dish.
5. Toss blueberries with sugar, cornstarch, and cinnamon.
6. Add to the dish.
7. Crumble the rest of the dough on top of the blueberries.
8. Bake for 45 minutes, cool, and serve.

Tips and Substitutions

- Cook meat in bulk and freeze in gallon bags for future meals.
- Warm serving dishes before adding hot food.
- When separating yolks from whites, always start in a separate small dish. The smallest bit of yolk will ruin any chances of whipping whites to peaks.
- When adding cornstarch to a dish, mix the desired amount in an equal amount of cold water or milk first. Adding cornstarch straight to a hot liquid will cause it to clump.
- Prick potatoes with a fork or knife before cooking.
- Coat your measuring cup with pan spray when measuring honey, peanut butter, or another sticky ingredient.
- Always pack brown sugar.
- Always use whole milk when cooking or baking.
- Always large room temperature eggs when baking.
- Soften butter by setting on the counter ½ hour before baking.
- Bread flour is best for bread but is not always necessary. All-purpose flour works very well for most flour needs.
- Adding ¼ tsp of vitamin C powder per 3 cups of flour helps bread rise faster and last longer.
- Coconut oil will save slightly burnt chocolate.
- Keep bouillon cubes or better than bullion paste for broth.
- A package of yeast is 2 ¼ tsp.
- Instant yeast and active yeast can be interchanged for each other, but active yeast needs more time to proof, and the dough needs more time to double.
- 100-110°F is the ideal water temperature for yeast.
- 120-130°F is the ideal water temperature for instant yeast.

- Stiff Peaks: whipped egg whites that keep their shape
- Cream: to work butter and sugar into a paste
- Brine: to soak in salty water. 1 tbl salt : 1 cup water
- Scant: just shy of the actual measurement
- Wash: a liquid brushed onto pastries for color and shine
  - 1 egg, 1 egg white, or 1 yolk mixed with 1 tbl of water for a wash on pastries

- When used as a thickening agent, 1 tbl cornstarch can be substituted for 2 tbls flour
- Honey and white sugar can be substituted for each other
- Mayonnaise can be substituted for oil in cakes
- Cinnamon sugar = 4 tbls sugar + 1 tbl ground cinnamon
- Garlic salt = 1 tbls salt + 1 tsp garlic powder
- Buttermilk = 1 tbl lemon juice + 1 cup milk
- Sour cream 1 cup = 6 oz. cream cheese + 2 tbls milk
- 1 egg = 1 tbl ground flax seed + 3 tbls water
- 1 egg = 1 tbl chia seeds + 2 ½ tbls water
- 1 egg = 3 tbls yogurt, cottage cheese, or sour cream

- Cream Soup:
  - 4 tbls butter
  - ¼ cup flour
  - 1 cup milk
  - 2 tsp bullion paste
  - ¼ tsp onion powder
  - ¼ tsp garlic powder
  - ¼ tsp salt
  - ¼ tsp pepper
  - ¼ tsp parsley flakes
  1. Melt butter in a saucepan and whisk in flour.
  2. Whisk in milk, bullion paste, and spices at a low heat until it is at desired thickness.
  3. Makes about 10 oz. or one can of cream soup.

1 Gallon	Ounces	Pounds	Cups	Tbl	Tsp	Fl oz	Pint	Quart	Liter
4 quarts			4 c	64 tbls	-	32 oz	2 pts	1 qt	950 ml
8 pints			2 c	32 tbls	-	16 oz	1 pt	½ qt	470 ml
16 cups			1 c	16 tbls	48 tsp	8 oz	½ pt	¼ qt	240 ml
128 fl oz			¾ c	12 tbls	36 tsp	6 oz	¼ pt	-	177 ml
3.8 liters			⅔ c	11 tbls	32 tsp	5 ⅓ oz	-	-	160 ml
			½ c	8 tbls	24 tsp	4 oz	-	-	120 ml
	1 oz	1/16 lb	⅓ c	5 tbls	16 tsp	2 ⅔ oz	-	-	80 ml
	2 oz	⅛ lb	¼ c	4 tbls	12 tsp	2 oz	-	-	60 ml
	4 oz	¼ lb	⅛ c	2 tbls	6 tsp	1 oz	-	-	30 ml
	8 oz	½ lb	-	1 tbl	3 tsp	½ oz	-	-	15 ml
	16 oz	1 lb							

Minimum Internal Meat Temperatures

Poultry – 165°F   Ground Meat – 165°F   Fish – 145°F

Beef, Lamb, Veal, Pork – 165°F (and rest for 3 min. before testing)

Printed in the USA
CPSIA information can be obtained
at www.ICGtesting.com
LVHW080737200923
758698LV00006B/113